THEATRE SKETCHBOOK

To my friends in the theatre

Claude Marks

THEATRE
SKETCHBOOK

AMBER LANE PRESS

Published in 1982 by
Amber Lane Press Ltd
9a Newbridge Road
Ambergate
Derbyshire DE5 2GR

ISBN 0 906399 33 5

Typeset by Input Typesetting Ltd., London
Printed and bound in Great Britain at
The Bowering Press, Plymouth.

Contents

My special thanks to all those who have kindly granted their permission for certain portraits in their possession to be reproduced in this book:

Mr and Mrs Richard Bullen, Frances Cuka, Mr and Mrs George Edge, Mr and Mrs Ben Edwards, Glenda Jackson and Roy Hodges, Mr and Mrs Brian W. Kaltner, Georgiana Morrison, Mrs Donald Oenslager, Mr and Mrs Marty Rosenthal, Joy L. Safran, Francis Warner, Mr and Mrs Philip W. Wilkinson.

The verse on page 47 is quoted with the kind permission of J. B. Priestley, O.M.

Foreword

The relationship between art and the theatre has always fascinated me. I came to painting through stage design, and I have great affection and admiration for such artists as Jacques Callot, Watteau, Hogarth, Daumier, Toulouse-Lautrec and Sickert who found inspiration in the world of the stage and who had a special empathy with performers. It is always a good idea to begin at the top, and I am glad that my first theatrical portrait drawings, in 1956, were of that legendary figure Edward Gordon Craig, who was trained as an actor under Henry Irving and whose ideas gave new freedom to scenic design.

Since I was born and grew up in London and have lived for many years in New York, I have had the good fortune to meet and draw outstanding theatre personalities on both sides of the Atlantic, sketching them in performance and offstage, in character and as themselves. This book is devoted mainly to British theatre people; another volume dealing mostly, but not exclusively, with American actors and producers, is in preparation.

When an actor poses in costume there is the challenge of interpreting both the underlying personality and the mask he or she has assumed for the role. Sketches made during a performance can, if successful, capture the essence of a production and of the individual characters. It is most gratifying to hear an actor say, "With a few lines you have expressed exactly what I was hoping to convey."

Claude Marks
New York, 1982

7

Edward Gordon Craig

My first drawings of a theatre personality were of Edward Gordon Craig, son of the great Ellen Terry, and a pioneer of modern stage design. I met him in the summer of 1956 when he was 84 and living in Vence in the hills near Nice. Even though few of his designs were ever executed, he was a legendary figure, and his influence was enormous.

When I was in Paris in the late 1930s, studying painting and stage design, the writer Léon Kochnitzky and I spent an entire evening looking for Gordon Craig, whom I was eager to meet. We dropped in at various Left Bank bars, restaurants and cafés that we knew he frequented but Craig had either just left or was expected to arrive soon. After an evening of frustration, we abandoned the search.

A series of radio talks by Craig recorded in Vence between 1951 and 1953 by the BBC for the Third Programme rekindled my interest in this extraordinary man.

He began by saying in a firm triumphant tone, "No, this is not a voice from the dead!" There was excitement in his voice as he recounted his early experiences as a young actor with his mother and Henry Irving in the great days of the Lyceum Theatre, his tours in the provinces, his meeting with the famous Italian actor Salvini (the outstanding Othello of his day) and as he described the personality and artistry of his great love, Isadora Duncan.

In the summer of 1956, when on a painting trip in southern France, I had written to Craig from Aix-en-Provence to ask if I might call on him in Vence. Since some friends were driving in that

Claude Mauks.
Vence: 1956
E.G.C.

10

direction, I left Aix with my wife and son before the answer had time to arrive.

In Vence it turned out that although everyone knew Monsieur Craig, no-one seemed to know his address. Some said he lived just outside Vence, others believed he had moved from Vence to the little village of Tourettes-sur-Loup, where there were *beaucoup d'artistes*. Post-office inquiries proved fruitless. Some instinct prompted me on our homeward journey in mid-afternoon to leave my family and friends in Grasse and take a bus back to Vence. Since the bus stopped for a few minutes in Tourettes, I eagerly scanned the little square. I suddenly saw, seated alone at a table in the *terrasse* of a deserted café, a lean, white-clad, white-haired old man with a lofty, wrinkled forehead, thoroughly absorbed in a game of solitaire. This could only be Gordon Craig. The bus was about to leave but I tore through the aisle, to the astonishment of the other passengers, and alighted just in time, realizing that I need seek no further.

"Excuse me, you *are* Mr. Craig?" I asked. He replied that indeed he was, and invited me to sit at his table. "You'll have to speak up. I don't hear very well," he added.

It took me some time to explain who I was, and why I was so eager to meet him. When I mentioned Léon Kochnitzky his face lit up, he remembered my letter, and said that he had written to me.

His attire and appearance were spectacular. Horn-rimmed spectacles were perched high on his forehead, and he wore a strange, white linen garment, doubtless of Craigian design, buttoned down the front, with upstanding collar—a cross between a shepherd's smock, a gardener's overall and a surgeon's operating coat. Folded over the left shoulder was a large, grey, toga-like wrap, which he draped around himself in the cool of the evening. Contrasting with all the whiteness and greyness was the thin black cord of his hearing aid. On the chair beside him was his wide-brimmed straw hat which, he told me, came from the Italian quarter in Nice. Later, when I saw him walking across the square, and pausing to chat

11

E.G.C.

Claude Marks
Vence. 1956

with various acquaintances, this tall, slightly stooped figure with
the wide-brimmed hat, the long white hair, the coat reaching to his
calves and the pale grey drapery, created an unforgettable image.

When alone, or in moments of repose or fatigue, his age became
apparent. But when he was in company, his features were mobile
and animated, his voice and gestures emphatic. His occasional
dogmatic outbursts were offset by an enthusiasm, an intellectual
curiosity, and a rather malicious sense of humour that conveyed a

Claude
Marks.
Vence. 1956

E.G.C.

feeling of youthful vigour. With his transparent skin, his blue-grey eyes with their heavy lids, his strong aquiline nose (reminiscent of his cousin Sir John Gielgud), and his thin-lipped, almost Voltairean mouth, he suggested now a venerable patriarch, now a sprightly old lady, now a petulant and mischievous schoolboy. A man of many moods and contradictory impulses, he was always colourful, always on the grand scale, always intensely alive.

He asked me various questions about my work for the theatre

and expressed a desire to see some designs, giving me the name and telephone number of his pension in Vence; I was to come for coffee at two o'clock the next day. "I won't ask you to lunch," he added, "the food is so abominable."

Owing to his deafness, conversation was still difficult. "Don't spit at me!" he exclaimed at one point, but I found that when I sat next to him instead of opposite him we could converse more easily. We were soon joined by an old friend of his, a pleasant, middle-aged Englishman who was a member of the art colony of Tourettes and a sculptor in plaster. After introducing me, Craig remarked, pointing to his friend, "*He* knows how to pitch his voice right. You see," he added with a wink, "he was trained as a clown!"

This led to a dissertation on a subject which fascinated Craig, and on which he had done abundant research—19th-century English farces, which were often presented on bills with more serious works, but following them, not as curtain-raisers. When he was a young member of Irving's company, Craig himself appeared in several of these comical pieces. However revolutionary Craig's ideas of staging were, his roots were in the late-Victorian theatre. He had, in fact, some of the characteristics of the old-time actor-manager.

While he was looking through an illustrated book that his friend had brought along, I made several sketches of him, using a new type of drawing pen made in Germany. He enquired about the pen and tried it himself, eager to know of every new invention. He said that in the old days he used to make many quick sketches in the London music-halls. When I asked him to sign one of my sketches of him, he inscribed: "By Marks, of E.G.C., [his florid monogram] here in Vence." Underneath he wrote, "Marks has the good—support him," and said, "There, you can show *that* to theatre managers if they're ever nasty to you!" The idea was intriguing but hardly realistic!

He asked me what I thought of marionettes. I knew how prominently masks and marionettes figured in the Craigian desire for a

15

more hieratic, symbolic, less realistic type of theatre. His conception of the actor as *Ubermarionette* was still being discussed in Paris, and I later learned that he had been working on a marionette play consisting of 365 scenes, and entitled *Drama for Fools*. I replied, "Well, I once did some designs for marionettes. . ." He replied testily, "That's not what I meant. That's the trouble with so many of you younger fellows nowadays. A little bit of this, a little bit of that. You've got to have *one* idea and go right after it."

He then went on to discuss the life-sized marionettes of Java. When I said that, to my knowledge, the Javanese plays were based on traditional legends and symbols that the public understood, he really exploded. Banging on the table with the flat of his right hand, he thundered with what Eleonora Duse long ago described as his *furor Britannicus*: "I don't give a *damn* what the public understands!"

Hastily changing the subject, I asked him what contemporary directors he believed had been most influenced by his ideas. He singled out London's Peter Brook, who had recently written an article on Craig in the *Sunday Times*. "Peter Brook wrote to me recently," said Craig, "asking me just how I imagined the island in *The Tempest*. And do you know, I couldn't think of an answer. What sort of an island *is* it?"

Craig was delighted that Queen Elizabeth II had made him a C. H. (Companion of Honour) earlier in the year, and felt that this may have had something to do with two articles on him appearing on the same day in the *Sunday Times* and the *Observer*, the latter by the drama critic Kenneth Tynan. "People will think it's a conspiracy!" he chuckled.

While regretting the meagreness of his income (inherited from his mother Ellen Terry), which prohibited the hiring of a secretary, and while resenting the fact that he had never had a real theatre of his own in which to realize his ideas, he did not, I felt, find his role of 'prophet-king-in-exile' altogether distasteful. At one point Craig wandered off across the square to find the elusive waiter. ("That waiter should really seek some other form of employment," he muttered angrily.) During his absence I asked his friend what it would have been like if Craig *had* been given the theatre of his dreams. "Shall I tell you?" he replied. "He would have been *hell!*"

At 6–15 it was time to catch the evening bus back to Vence. The conductor was standing in the doorway of the bus, chatting with the driver, and Craig exclaimed irritably in English (he had never bothered to learn even passable French after years of residence): "Either get inside or get off, but don't just stand there blocking the entrance!" We made our way to our seats and the sculptor friend waved goodbye. When the conductor came around to collect the fare, Craig remarked to me, rather in the manner of a belligerent English tourist of 1860, "You had better count your change—they're a bunch of robbers!" He got off at his pension and waved gaily as the bus drove back into the centre of Vence. I was delighted but somewhat exhausted by this first meeting.

The following afternoon, after selecting my designs carefully and somewhat apprehensively, I set out with my wife and son for Craig's pension. We found him sitting in the garden. He was in his most gracious, charming mood, and in his outlandish French he ordered three coffees, and a Coca-Cola for the boy. He asked David, then twelve years old, whether he too would take up the theatre. David replied that while he loved the theatre he preferred sailing. "Ah, that's fine," said Craig. "Perhaps you can do both! The Duke of Edinburgh, now, he's quite a sailor, isn't he? And that young Queen, she's doing a fine job." He beamed appreciatively, thinking perhaps of his recent honour. "Generally speaking, though," he went on, talking to all of us, "the women of England haven't done nearly enough for the arts. Not that I'm against women mind you. I adore women!"

I told him how intrigued I had been as a child by a photograph in an illustrated Shakespeare of himself as the ailing King Edward IV in *Richard III*. "Ah yes," he replied, "that was the last play I ever appeared in with Irving. And that was the only time I ever saw Irving [playing Richard] on his knees before me." Craig recalled the

17

strenuousness of those early theatrical days, including one season in Hereford when he was called upon, at very short notice, to play Hamlet, Romeo and Charles Surface on successive nights.

Among modern actors, Olivier was obviously his favourite. Craig had seen him just after World War II, in Paris, in *Richard III*, and also as Oedipus and Mr Puff (in *The Critic*), the last two performances being given on the same evening. But Craig did not have occasion to see many plays. He had not seen Gielgud on the stage in more than twenty years.

I asked him if he had had much contact with Bernard Shaw. "We just met once or twice," he replied. "He was always generous, never mean or petty. But what I could not bear was his making love to actresses in order to get them to act in his plays!"

Craig asked to see my designs. He examined every sketch and photograph very carefully, asking many questions. At one point, looking through the portfolio, he remarked, "Well, this all seems personal, I don't see any influences," meaning, perhaps, that he could not find much of *his* influence; for on seeing a project for Shelley's *The Cenci* (never carried out), which was conceived in a more austere manner than the rest, he exclaimed, "Ah, that's a bit Craigy!"

As he looked through the designs, my wife took a series of snapshots. He then posed for two photographs, wearing his wonderful hat. In the first he was smiling benignly, his chin cupped in his massive hand. In the other his head was thrown back with a jaunty expression, his left hand poised against his chest—very much the 'Grand Old Actor'. When I sent him prints of these last two snapshots he liked the first one but objected to the second on the ground that it made him look 'conceited'. "And," he added disarmingly in his letter, "you didn't find me conceited, *did* you?"

Before we left, Craig invited David and me to his room—he would not ask my wife, owing to its disorder. The room was so crowded with books, magazines, correspondence (from Irving, Stanislavsky, Duse, and others), drawings, photographs and me-

Claude
Marks
Vence, 1956

mentos, that we could hardly move. On the wall, high up, were some stylized masks of his own making. A fine, framed drawing for the ghost in *Hamlet* attracted my attention, and he showed me some massive, rare editions of books containing his designs— sweeping, imaginative conceptions, but always with a keen eye for scale and for technical detail. His books and newspaper clippings were full of underlinings and marginal notes in his fine, nervous handwriting.

Claude
Marks
Venu, 1956

Out of a pile of photographs he selected three, one for each of us. He gave David a photograph of himself aged four or five (signed "EGC, 1876–7?")—a blond, chubby infant seated with great assurance astride a fluted classical column, riding whip in hand. For my wife he had chosen a delightful picture dated 1885, which showed him at thirteen as the gardener's boy in Irving's production of *Eugene Aram*. (This had been Craig's only visit to America.) The third photograph must have been taken in the late 1940s, and had a wonderful Dickensian quality. Craig wore a wide-brimmed black felt hat and a handsomely draped woollen cloak – he had a gaily militant air. On it he inscribed: "Claude Marks from Gordon Craig, Vence, August, 1956."

By now he was ready for his siesta and we took our leave. My last glimpse was of Gordon Craig seated in his straight-backed armchair among all his papers, all his memories. He looked very old, very tired. When I expressed the hope that our visit had not fatigued him, he replied, "Oh no, it's just old age, my boy, old age." But he said with a twinkle as we went out of the room, "Let me know where you are and what sceneries [*sic*] you are doing."

I never saw Gordon Craig again but we corresponded for several years. When the United Scenic Artists' Union decided to make him an honorary member in celebration of his 89th birthday in 1961, I wrote to Craig asking his permission. He replied giving his consent but adding, with typical mock-testiness, "Don't waste a lot of time standing around making speeches and drinking my health!"

The ceremony was duly held, on the small stage of the Neighborhood Playhouse, and many came to pay tribute. A presentation plaque was sent to Craig in Vence, together with transcripts of the speeches and photographs of the event. He was pleased by the gesture but could not resist commenting in a letter to me that one of the main speeches was ". . . much too long and very boring."

Soon afterwards I learned that, by selling the bulk of his remarkable theatrical collection to the Bibliothèque Nationale in Paris, Craig was able to move out of his cramped pension to more

21

comfortable quarters. He was cared for in his last years by his daughter Nelly. He died on the morning of July 29, 1966, aged 94.

This great innovator of the theatre was a subtle and complex man, who cannot be summed up in any one phrase. But his eternally youthful spirit was wittily conveyed in a statement by Sir Henry Irving's grandson and biographer, Laurence Irving, who described Edward Gordon Craig as ". . . the most venerable beatnik of them all."

E.G.C.
Vence, 1956

Claude
Marks

All of the drawings in this chapter were done in the summer of 1956 in Vence, southern France, when Gordon Craig was 84.

John Gielgud

Three years had gone by since I had sketched Gordon Craig in Vence. In September 1959, when I was living in New York at the Chelsea Hotel, another illustrious member of the Terry family, Sir John Gielgud—referred to in one of Craig's letters as 'Cousin John'—was appearing on Broadway as Benedick in the U.S. tour of his own production of *Much Ado About Nothing*.

Ever since my schooldays in England I had admired the style, grace and lyric passion that Gielgud brought to his roles. His performance as the wayward, ill-fated king in *Richard of Bordeaux* in 1933 was an unforgettable experience, and as a Cambridge undergraduate I made special trips to London to see his Hamlet, as well as his Mercutio in the famous production of *Romeo and Juliet* in which he and Laurence Olivier alternated the roles of Romeo and Mercutio.

My first meeting with Gielgud was in 1956 when I called on him at his home in Cowley Street in Westminster to pick up a portfolio of my set and costume designs that I had left for him to see. They included designs for Joan Littlewood's production of *An Italian Straw Hat*.

Gielgud was friendly and encouraging, with his characteristic blend of cordiality and shyness, volubility and reserve. I noticed a painting by Christopher Wood on the wall, among other works of art and mementos. I remember him saying, referring to *The Good Soldier Schweik*, "Joan Littlewood's a clever producer, but I don't think theatre and politics should mix."

While sailing back to New York on a freighter in the autumn of

1956, I wrote an article on my visit to Craig which was published in September of the following year in *Theatre Arts* magazine, illustrated by my sketches and a photograph taken by my wife. Now, two years later, I left the article at the theatre where *Much Ado* was playing, with a note asking Sir John if he would have time to pose for me at the Chelsea. To my delight he accepted.

Having inherited a rather impressive Victorian armchair from the one-man show by Hal Holbrook, *Mark Twain Tonight*, I decided that this would be most suitable to accommodate Sir John. I waited in the lobby of the hotel; at the appointed time Gielgud strode in 'incognito' wearing dark glasses and elegantly dressed.

Arriving in the studio, and noticing sketches and photographs of Gordon Craig on the mantelpiece, he launched immediately, without preliminaries, into a stream of staccato, densely concentrated remarks and observations: "That was a good article on Craig—the drawings were good too—he looks very Voltairean—did you notice those strangler's thumbs?—looks rather like a woman, always did, his sister was quite mannish—" I pointed out with amusement Craig's flamboyant inscription beneath one of my sketches of him, "Marks has the good—support him." Gielgud replied, "Oh, that's typical, so patronizing; when he came to London he invited me to lunch at the Café Royal, ordered champagne, terribly condescending. . ."

It was a hot September afternoon. Before stepping onto the model stand Gielgud removed his jacket and tie. He wore a sage-green shirt with large and distinctive cuff-links. He took his place in the armchair, and with his innate visual sense he seemed to know at once what kind of pose would be most interesting. At regular intervals, and without being asked, he would uncross his legs and take up, another, equally interesting position. The time-span in each case was sufficient for me to obtain a satisfactory

John Gielgud sketched in black conté crayon in the artist's studio
at the Chelsea Hotel, New York, 1959.

Claude Marks
Sept. 29, 1959
New York

25

John Gielgud as the Headmaster in Alan Bennett's
Forty Years On, *at the Apollo Theatre, London, 1968.*

John Gielgud as Spooner in No Man's Land
by Harold Pinter, New York, 1976.

drawing. Meanwhile he kept up a fascinating, non-stop flow of conversation, pausing only when I was working on the face.

"You ought to draw Kenneth Tynan, he looks like Beardsley— you know what he said about my Benedick?—he wrote in his review that it was a cross between Malvolio and a lean, wet fox—ha!— ha!—ha!—he's awfully political, you know. . ."

I asked him about other portraits he had posed for. "Epstein started a bust of me, he never finished it, he'd liked my Hamlet and Richard II, but then he saw me in *Richard of Bordeaux* and found it too pretty-pretty and lost interest. I've sometimes thought of having Graham Sutherland do my portrait, but it might be rather alarming—all those crevices in my face. . ."

I said, and I meant it, "But Sir John, you have an age-less quality." He replied, "Oh well, all actors try to cultivate that."

27

John Gielgud
" Noah Curatti"
1978

Claude
Marks
1978

28

There were interesting contrasts in Gielgud's appearance—a real challenge for the draughtsman: the sensitive, mobile features and the rather stiff body, the long arms and the large, powerful hands. I selected three drawings to show him, one in black conté crayon, two in pen and ink. He remarked, "I find them charming." One was in profile, and he said, "It looks like Delius, I've been told I look like Delius."

My wife and son came down from our upstairs apartment to greet Sir John. Sue gave him one of the photographs she had taken of Craig—the one with his head thrown back, smiling, his hand placed jauntily on his chest. Gielgud loved it and said, "A real *cabotin* (the French word meaning, roughly, 'ham actor'). When we visited Gielgud backstage the following week, after his delightful *Much Ado*, we saw that he had attached the photograph to his dressing-room mirror. Since then he has reproduced the portrait in two of his books: *Distinguished Company* and *An Actor and His Time*.

There is a curious epilogue to this story: the venerable Mark Twain armchair collapsed under my very next sitter (fortunately an understanding acquaintance). No harm resulted, apart from the momentary shock. I sighed with relief at the thought of how narrowly I had escaped a mortifying experience! The chair had evidently fulfilled its destiny.

John Gielgud as Noel Cunliffe in Half-Life
by Julian Mitchell, London, 1978.

Ralph Richardson, New York, 1963.

Ralph Richardson

"Plagues and tortures! Can't I make her angry either? Oh, I am the most miserable fellow! But I'll not bear her presuming to keep her temper. No! She may break my heart, but she *shan't* keep her temper!"

I can still hear the ringing tones of Sir Ralph Richardson in the role of Sir Peter Teazle as his voice rose to what I can only describe as a 'crescendo-vibrato' at the close of Act II of *The School for Scandal*. An elegant, star-studded production of Sheridan's comedy had come to New York from London on a U.S. tour in the winter of 1962, and I saw it in February of the following year at the Majestic Theatre on Broadway. The direction was by John Gielgud, who also played the hypocritical Joseph Surface (a part he had last performed in 1937). Gielgud had aimed at bringing out the human reality in the play instead of resorting to stylish high camp or gimmicky updating for contemporary 'relevance'.

When the play opened at the Haymarket in London, in April 1962, some critics found Sir Ralph 'too likable' and insufficiently irascible, which made Lady Teazle, played in London by Anna Massey, seem rather cruel. But Caryl Brahms, in her review in *Plays and Players*, quoted Charles Lamb, who declared that, "Sir Peter Teazle must be no longer the comic idea of a fretful old bachelor bridegroom. He must be a real person . . . his suffering under his unfortunate match must have the downright pungency of life. . . ." In his New York performance Sir Ralph conveyed the vulnerability beneath the testiness and, without any loss to the comedy, won sympathy for the predicament of a basically warm-hearted man.

I left a note for Sir Ralph asking if he would pose for me as Sir Peter. Within a few days I received an amiable letter which, with its curlicued capitals, florid but neat script, and carefully spaced margins, deserved framing as a unique piece of penmanship. He agreed to pose one evening before the show.

Sir Ralph has made a practice in London, and in later visits to New York in 1970 and 1976, of arriving at the theatre at high speed on a motor-cycle, complete with crash helmet. This has caused some trepidation over the years but fortunately no mishaps. Whether or not this was his mode of transportation in 1963, his dressing-room at the Majestic Theatre had some of the 18th-century aura of the play. He had completed his make-up and was putting on his powdered wig. His dresser and valet was re-arranging the contents of a large hamper with some of Sir Ralph's personal effects. There were champagne glasses on the floor nearby. I was reminded of a genial, slightly eccentric English 'milord' of the time of George III, making the Grand Tour with his silver plate and choice wines to relieve the journey.

Before Sir Ralph began to pose I showed him photostats of my drawings of Gordon Craig, John Gielgud and other theatre person-alities. I knew that drawing was his hobby. His father had been a painter, and as a boy he too had wanted to be an artist. He had briefly attended art school in Brighton, but admitted to an inter-viewer that that had been 'a disaster'. He said to me at one point, "You know what I like to do sometimes? I like to stand in the wings during the scenes when I'm not on, and draw the shadows." Some-how the drawing of shadows rather than solid shapes seemed to fit the 'out-of-this-world', trance-like quality that Sir Ralph brings to some of his performances, and which is one aspect of his person-ality. But beneath his apparent vagueness and diffused but genuine benevolence there is shrewd observation. Those who know him well have remarked on his wide range of interests.

He posed as Sir Peter Teazle with one hand placed gracefully on his lace cravat, very much 'in period'. I had almost finished the

Ralph Richardson as Sir Peter Teazle in Sheridan's The
School for Scandal, *at the Majestic Theatre, New York, 1963.*

Ralph Richardson as Jack in Home *by David Storey, at the Morosco Theatre, New York, 1970.*

drawing when Gielgud looked in; he smiled as he saw the portrait in progress. Sir Ralph and I both took a rest, and he temporarily removed his wig. He said to Gielgud, "That was a nice drawing he did of you, Johnny," and Gielgud, his memory as precise as a Swiss watch, replied, "Yes, he did me four years ago."

As they chatted I made another sketch of Sir Ralph, without the wig and wearing glasses, but still looking like an affable 18th-century squire. Gielgud retailed some item of New York gossip which I cannot now recall, and left. Sir Ralph put on his wig and I finished the first drawing, which he signed in his ornate but controlled handwriting, adding the date: 1 Mar '63. He remarked of the portrait, "You know, it has something of old Sam Johnson!"

Ralph Richardson as Hirst in Harold Pinter's No Man's Land, *with John Gielgud as Spooner, in the National Theatre production, London, 1975.*

Since then I have made performance sketches of Sir Ralph when he has appeared with his longtime friend John Gielgud. Totally different in temperament, they complement each other admirably. It was a joy to see their subtly modulated performances in David Storey's moving and compassionate play *Home*, in 1970. Only gradually did one realize that Jack and Harry, with their dignified gentility, were, like the two plebeian female characters (brilliantly played by Mona Washbourne and Dandy Nichols), mental patients, and that the 'home' was an institution. They were equally effective in Harold Pinter's enigmatic *No Man's Land* in 1975, with Richardson's befuddled, apoplectic author Hirst being confronted in his plush Hampstead home by the disquieting intruder, Gielgud's rumpled, seedy poet and hanger-on, Spooner. "Isn't it a lark?" said Gielgud afterwards in high spirits; the two knights were obviously enjoying their venture into the strange world of Pinter.

Before the 1960s I had seen Ralph Richardson mainly in films. I remember especially his delightful tipsy scene in *The Divorce of Lady X* in 1938 (in which he co-starred with Laurence Olivier and Merle Oberon), and his sensitive portrayal of the butler Baines with little Bobby Henrey in *The Fallen Idol*. He has said in interviews that film gives him less satisfaction than theatre work, and he is also aware that on the stage he has had more success with character roles—Falstaff, Caliban, Bottom, Malvolio—than with the heroic Shakespearean parts. I regret not having seen his Peer Gynt and Cyrano. He brings a warm human perception to his roles, moving easily from comedy to pathos. Even when he portrays 'ordinary men' he invests them with a strangeness and oddity that are sometimes a reaction to unusual circumstances but which in a larger sense reflect the unpredictability of life.

In his offstage personality Sir Ralph is cordial and generous but not easy to grasp: there is a curious almost Dickensian touch of fantasy contrasting with his practical, commonsense side. Clive Revill told me that once, after returning from a holiday abroad, he met Sir Ralph taking a walk in Hampstead. Clive told him that he had just been on vacation. Sir Ralph looked at Clive and said with wonderment, "So I see—you're as *brown* as a *berry* . . . as *brown* as a *berry*. . ." As he turned and walked away, Clive could still hear him repeating to himself in a melodious diminuendo. . ." as brown as a berry . . . as brown as a berry. . ."

Sybil Thorndike

"She has the eyes of a sixteen-year-old girl." This was the comment of an American actress friend on seeing one of my portrait drawings of Sybil Thorndike, whose friendship I treasured over a period of ten years. Since we were so soon on a first name basis, I shall refer to her as Sybil.

Although I did not meet her until 1966 when she was an energetic 84, my memories of her go back to the first Shakespeare plays I saw in London as a child. I remember her entrance as Lady Macbeth, wearing an orange headband, in a production stunningly designed by Charles Ricketts. She was perusing Macbeth's letter, and I can still hear her firm, clear tones as she read the opening lines, "They met me in the day of success. . ." Then there was her moving, dignified Queen Catherine, regal in ermine and velvet, in a lavish production of *Henry VIII* in 1925. I had no inkling at the time that Laurence Olivier was assistant stage manager as well as playing the First Serving Man!

Sybil's sense of comedy and her sheer high spirits were evident in *The Taming of the Shrew*, with her husband Lewis Casson as Petruchio. When Shaw's *St. Joan* was revived in the early 1930s, with Ricketts' superlative sets and costumes, I admired her down-to-earth yet exalted Joan. My own mental picture of the Maid of Orleans was somewhat different, but I could see why Bernard Shaw had written the play with her in mind.

While I am aware that Sybil's versatility extended to broad comedy and *Grand Guignol*, I unfortunately never saw her in those kinds of role. Among her stage appearances in London in the 1950s, I

Sybil Thorndike and Lewis Casson, London, 1965.

Claude marks
London 1965

particularly remember her Mrs Whyte, the 'aristocratic lady who has known better days', in N. C. Hunter's play *Waters of the Moon*. It opened in 1951 at the Haymarket Theatre and was still running nearly two years later. The cast featured another 'great lady' of the stage, Dame Edith Evans, as the volatile, flamboyant Helen Doncaster.

Sybil was delighted at the opportunity the part gave her to play the piano in the climactic New Year's Eve Party scene in the lonely Devonshire hotel where the action takes place. Music was always her great passion, and I later learned that her early hopes for a career as a concert pianist had been dashed before the age of eighteen by agonizing wrist pains. It was then that she took up acting.

In *Waters of the Moon* she remained, in the earlier phases of the party scene, the 'intelligent and slightly soured' widow, occasionally making tart replies to the other guests, or else sitting silently on a settee, interminably knitting, a sad, resigned spectator whom life had passed by (the complete antithesis of the real Sybil). After making querulous objections to the loud jazz music on the radio that the young people wanted to dance to, she suddenly announced, mellowed by a few glasses of champagne, "If you wish to dance, I will play for you."

One could feel the excitement in the audience as Mrs Whyte moved, a little unsteadily, toward the piano and sat down to play. Sybil's exquisite rendering of some Chopin waltzes will be remembered by all who heard it; in terms of the play, it revealed, without a hint of sentimentality, the deep feeling beneath Mrs Whyte's bitterness and reserve. Sybil told her biographer Elizabeth Sprigge that the eminent pianist Dame Myra Hess was out front one night and came backstage afterwards to tell her that she was a 'great artist', and that no tribute had ever meant more to her.

Stage marriages, when they work, can be wonderful. I sensed the unique rapport between Lewis and Sybil when they gave a recital at the YMHA in New York in the late 1950s. Sybil was then about 75 and Lewis seven years older. As Lewis sat somewhat stiffly in his chair, stage right, reading in his deep, resonant voice, from Browning's *My Last Duchess*, it was a joy to see Sybil, who must have heard it many times before, seated stage left in her long recital gown, watching him admiringly and listening intently with her engaging, crooked smile. This was not the fixed, plastic smile of so many politicians' wives, but an expression of true appreciation and affection. It was hard not to keep one's eyes on her, although that was certainly not her intention.

In 1965 I had a large exhibition of my drawings, entitled *The American and English Theatre*, at the U.S. Embassy in London. I realized that without her portrait the show had been incomplete, and I was determined to include her in my next exhibit. Returning to London later that year, after a trip to Greece, I decided to make contact. It was characteristic of the Cassons that they did not have an unlisted phone number. I rang them, Lewis answered, and responded most cordially to my request that I come and sketch

Sybil Thorndike, London, 1966.

them. Within a couple of days I arrived at their flat in Swan's Court, just off the King's Road, Chelsea.

It was a cluttered but comfortable, 'lived-in' apartment. Full bookshelves flanked the mantelpiece, several paintings (one a Spanish landscape), and drawings, collected on their travels, hung on the walls, and there was a large globe of the world on a stand in the corner by the radio. Within a few minutes I felt completely at home.

41

Sybil, although most cooperative as a model, was not easy to draw. In spite of her strong bone-structure, less clearly defined, it is true, than in her younger days, she had the kind of face that needed to be seen in animation. That is why sculptured busts of her, including the one in the foyer of the Thorndike Theatre in Leatherhead, have a hard, fixed, 'set' expression which does not convey her personality. Dissatisfied with my first efforts, I found that I was more successful drawing her when she was listening to music on the radio—Bach was a special favourite. Then her features had a gentle, inward quality, for music appealed to her deepest sensibilities—but even that was a different look from her expression when responding to people or to an amusing situation, an expression that I was finally able to capture some years later when watching her on a television interview. When I showed her that sketch, she exclaimed, "Oh, you *clever* boy!", a cheering remark to one not in his first youth!

Sybil enjoyed posing and was candid in her reactions. Of one of the earlier drawings she said, "My nose is straighter than that – it's a *good* nose!" As I was sketching Lewis with his high, domed forehead and deceptively stern expression, she remarked, not about the drawing but about the subject, "Doesn't he look *fierce*?"

With her outgoing, generous nature, Sybil tended to see, and bring out, the best in everyone. However, she could react sharply to anything that seemed to her pretentious or unprofessional. I told her of my meetings with Gordon Craig, and she remarked, "Craig was a *conceited* man. Now people used to think Shaw was conceited, but he really wasn't – he was genuinely modest, in fact rather shy. But Craig – now *he* was conceited." About an actress less than half her age whom I had seen in a repertory company, she said, "She's a nice old stick, but she hasn't much talent!"

The last time I saw Lewis and Sybil performing together was in a London production of *Arsenic and Old Lace* in 1966. Sybil and Athene Seyler were the eccentric old ladies who, out of pity for lonely, elderly gentlemen, poison them with their own concoction

Sybil Thorndike as Abby Brewster in Kesselring's Arsenic and Old Lace, *at the Vaudeville Theatre, London, 1966.*

Claude
Merbs
1966

of elderberry wine. Lewis, aged 90 (a fact noted in the programme), played the Superintendent of the Mental Home who comes in at the end to take the ladies away and gets poisoned himself. He played the role with relish and, to the audience's delight, clambered nimbly up a flight of stairs and came down a moment later carrying parcels. When I went to the stage door after the matinée, I was touched when the doorman said, "The old ladies are taking their nap." There was that 'family' feeling, typical of a certain aspect of the British theatre.

One afternoon in the summer of 1968 I rang the Cassons' doorbell as usual and I heard Sybil cheerily humming as she came to open the door. She apologized that Lewis was not there to greet me and explained that he was taking his siesta. Then, leaning towards me, she added, in a conspiratorial stage whisper, "You know, he doesn't take kindly to old age!" She herself was a mere 86!

I never saw Lewis again. He died in May 1969, after a marriage that had lasted over sixty years. Sybil showed admirable courage and resilience, and, despite increasing trouble with arthritis, continued to fulfil all her engagements, including broadcasts, recitals and TV appearances. She was tireless in her support, never dogmatic, for progressive causes. I regret not having seen her in *There Was an Old Woman* at the Thorndike Theatre in Leatherhead in the autumn of 1969, in which she gave a hilarious performance as one of 'those old girls you see sitting around on steps and benches'—she was on stage throughout the play.

To my great delight she agreed, in September 1970, to open an exhibition of my theatre drawings at 'The Room', a charming gallery in Greenwich run by Roy Hodges (at that time married to Glenda Jackson). Sybil said, "I look forward to seeing your work *en masse*."

On the day of the opening, Roy arranged for Sybil to be driven out to Greenwich and taken home in a limousine. A beautiful wicker armchair with a high, arched back, was installed in the gallery for her comfort. Before taking her place in the armchair, Sybil insisted on my giving her a conducted tour of the exhibition and showing her every drawing. "Who's that dear child?" she asked, looking at my sketch of the gifted black New York actress Cicely Tyson. She saw her own portrait and paused for a moment in front of the Emlyn Williams drawing, fondly recalling her appearance with him years before in his play *The Corn is Green*. When she came to my sketches of the hippie musical *Hair*, then running in London, a slight edge came into her voice: "I don't know *why* people would want to go to the theatre to see a lot of bare backs!"

Sybil bought my sketch of Glenda Jackson ("such a talented young actress") as Charlotte Corday; and her grand-daughter Diana Devlin chose a signed performance sketch of John Gielgud, standing dejectedly, centre stage, at the very end of David Storey's play *Home*. With his characteristic turn of phrase, Sir John had said when I showed him the sketch, "You've captured my stance."

The opening was most enjoyable. Glenda made a brief appearance with her new baby, Danny, and Harold Pinter came with his wife Vivien Merchant. But it was Sybil's presence that made the occasion truly memorable. William Hickey's column in the *Daily Express* noted, "Most of the senior members of her profession such as Sir Laurence Olivier and Sir Alec Guinness who have their portraits hanging there were still unborn when Dame Sybil made her acting debut in Cambridge 66 years ago." I was pleased that the exhibition was later shown in the Thorndike Theatre, Leatherhead.

My last visit with Sybil was in early June 1976, a week before she died. I knew that she had been ailing but her housekeeper assured me that although she spent much time in bed she would be happy to see me. I went with my friend Frances Cuka, who had played Becky Sharp to Sybil's Miss Crawley in a musical version of *Vanity Fair* in 1962. Sybil was lying in bed looking serene and radiant. Her voice was faint, but she did not seem to be in pain, and her eyes were bright and responsive as ever. As she looked at the sunshine outside and then considered her bed-ridden state she exclaimed, "Oh, it's such a *damn* nuisance!"

Sybil Thorndike, London, 1971.

46

I gave her a copy of my son David's book, *Very Willing Griffin*, describing his crossing the Atlantic in a 19-foot boat in the solo transatlantic race of 1972 – I knew that her son John loved the sea and had joined the merchant navy as a young man – and I told her that David, alone out in the Atlantic, had been so happy to switch on his radio and hear her in *Desert Island Discs* on the BBC. We did not stay long, not wishing to tire her. Although we knew, as we kissed her goodbye, that we would not see her again, we left with a feeling of warmth and happiness.

Walking through crowded Westminster Abbey in 1980 I came across Sybil's commemorative tablet set in the flagstones near the choir, with the moving poem by J. B. Priestley, ending:

> And now the scripts lie fading
> on the shelf,
> We celebrate your finest
> role—Yourself;
> The calls, the lights grow dim
> but not this part,
> The Christian Spirit,
> The Great Generous Heart.

While these lines evoked many memories, the words that remind me most vividly of Sybil's joy in her work and her boundless zest for life, are those I heard so often in the intimacy of Swan's Court, "Oh, we had such *fun* with that, didn't we, Lewis?"

Frances Cuka, New York, 1961.

Frances Cuka

She can play a gamine or Goneril, a sensitive waif or a slatternly landlady. On stage she can look glamorous or dowdy, and portray any age from sixteen to sixty-five. Besides being an extremely gifted and versatile actress, Frances Cuka is a delightful person, generous, companionable, buoyant and good-tempered even under trying circumstances, and with a quick but never malicious sense of humour.

To those meeting her for the first time the initial impression is often that of a voluble extrovert but further acquaintance reveals that beneath her natural exuberance there is keen perception, shrewd, practical common sense, a strong capacity for friendship, and a wide range of cultural interests.

It was indirectly through my association with Joan Littlewood's Theatre Workshop in London in 1955 that I first met Frances in New York six years later. I received a letter from Joan suggesting that I contact an American friend of hers, a folk-singer, in New York. At a party given by this lady, in April 1961, my wife Sue and I were introduced to Frances.

She was small and full of vitality, her features piquant rather than conventionally pretty. She would make, I felt, a wonderful subject for drawing and painting. After the party we accompanied Frances to her midtown hotel. As sometimes happens in these situations, we hardly ever saw our hostess again, but Frances became a close friend and has remained so over the years.

Shortly after this first meeting we saw Frances as Jo in *A Taste of Honey* at the Booth Theatre on Broadway. She had originally created the role at the Theatre Royal, Stratford East, in May 1958, and brought a mixture of tough cheekiness and vulnerability, tender poetry and earthy realism to the part that made one feel that here was a survivor, however hopeless her situation. Only in the final moments, when she was alone in the dismal room with her baby, repeating the words of the plaintive little song—As I was going up Pippin Hill, Pippin Hill was dirty—only then did the sadness come through.

I was haunted by this performance for several years, and in the first drawings for which Frances posed at the Chelsea Hotel, and for some time afterwards, the 'Taste of Honey syndrome' persisted. Sometimes her expression in the sketches was humorous, at other times pensive, but a waif-like quality, slightly reminiscent of Fellini's wife Giulietta Massina in his films *La Strada* and *Nights of Cabiria*, kept surfacing. One drawing was in black conté crayon, others were in pen and ink; a large pastel and ink study on brown paper was exhibited at my first large New York show at the FAR Gallery in 1961.

Frances posed often and willingly. She has a highly developed visual sense and some artistic talent. She told me that in her childhood in Brighton her father had given her an easel and oils and encouraged her to paint and draw. But she soon realized that acting was her vocation and she studied for the stage at the Guildhall School of Music and Drama in London.

Her joining the Theatre Workshop Company led to appearances in Zürich and at the Moscow Art Theatre in Joan Littlewood's production of *Macbeth*. Between her success at the Theatre Royal in *A Taste of Honey* and her New York debut in the same play, she had an exciting succession of roles, including the slovenly Daffodil in John Arden's social comedy *Live Like Pigs*, and Nell (visible only from the neck up) in Beckett's *End Game*.

There followed a brilliant Shakespearean season at Stratford-on-Avon with the Royal Shakespeare Company. Frances remembers with particular pleasure playing Jessica to Peter O'Toole's splendid Shylock (the best she has ever seen) and the experience

Frances Cuka as Jo in A Taste of Honey *by Shelagh
Delaney, at the Booth Theatre, New York, 1962.*

of moving from the lusty Maria in *Twelfth Night* to the baleful
Cassandra in *Troilus and Cressida*. Having heard her recite excerpts
from Racine's *Phèdre*, I can imagine the power and intensity that
she must have brought to Cassandra's dire prophetic utterances.

Since I was living in New York and visiting London mostly in
the summer I inevitably missed a number of Frances's performances, including her Becky Sharp in a 1962 musical version of *Vanity
Fair*, with Dame Sybil Thorndike as Miss Crawley.

By 1968, when I saw her as Marcelle, the sad, ignorant little
Parisian tart in *Days in the Trees* by Marguerite Duras, at the Aldwych Theatre, Frances was appearing quite regularly with the Royal

Frances Cuka, London, 1968.

Clande
Marks
1969

Shakespeare Company. Her robust sense of comedy and her colourful mezzo-soprano must have made her Lucy Lockitt in *The
Beggar's Opera* in late 1968 at the Apollo Theatre a delight.

One of her most challenging roles was that of Ellen in Harold
Pinter's *Silence*. This play was part of a double bill, with *Landscape*,
directed by Peter Hall, that I saw at the Aldwych in the summer of
1969. Frances found the role ". . . quite difficult to do but also very
rewarding." The three characters in the play—a woman and two
men—were lonely old people, living in their own rooms. They had
their own thoughts and different rhythms. Without benefit of
make-up or any change in physical appearance they had to suggest
the movement back and forth in time, from old age to youth.

Frances said of the experience, "It was a process of *thinking* myself old—using broad brushstrokes to make an instant impact."

In the same season at the Aldwych Frances was in less rarefied territory as the browbeaten Mrs Foran in Sean O'Casey's *The Silver Tassie*. With her shabby appearance and working-class Dublin accent she created such a vivid character that in my sketch of her made during performance I was at last able to break away from the 'Taste of Honey' image.

Frances's most avant-garde venture was in Ionesco's *Macbett*, a paradoxical transposition of *Macbeth*. I saw it at the Bankside Globe in London in 1973. Frances recalls, "I played Lady Duncan to start with. She got rather peculiar and attempted to seduce Macbett. Then I played the First Witch. Assisted by the Second Witch I did a strip-tease. I ended up in a wonderful sequinned number, which Macbett tore off. Then I was in a Barbarella costume, with a huge wig and false eyelashes. With stripper music playing I tempted Macbett —it was rather like the Devil tempting Christ."

In 1975 Frances played Lenin's wife, the drab, earnest Nadya Krupskaya, in *Travesties* by Tom Stoppard. Anyone who had not previously met her would have had the greatest difficulty in connecting the character they had seen on stage with the ebullient red-headed real-life Frances. She says, "I was always a tremendous puzzle. At the Aldwych everyone knew me. But when we moved to the New Theatre everyone was wondering who this redhead was, who came in, didn't appear to do anything, and then went out after the curtain! In the play I had this ash-blonde wig, very tight and with a severe bun at the back, and a shapeless, khaki-drab costume." Frances had the same trouble when the play transferred to New York later that year.

However, it was during the American run of *Travesties* that Frances was able to pose for me again. I painted her wearing an enormous black wide-brimmed hat of 1910 vintage that she had found in a friend's boutique. She wore it on the homeward flight and it almost touched the two sides of the plane!

Frances Cuka in her enormous black hat: oil on canvas, New York, 1975.

*Frances Cuka: portrait in water colour
and ink, New York, 1980.*

In London in 1952 I had seen a memorable production of N. C. Hunter's neo-Chekhovian play *Waters of the Moon* at the Haymarket Theatre. In a most satisfying link with the past, Frances appeared in the same play at the same theatre in 1978. She was playing the part that Wendy Hiller had played in 1951, and Wendy Hiller was playing Mrs Whyte, the role that Sybil Thorndike had created.

I asked Frances how Wendy Hiller had reacted to having her original role taken over. She replied, "Wendy was delightful. She left me totally alone, for which I was extremely grateful. At first we were terribly *nice* to each other, so anxious not to tread on each other's toes that we smiled a lot. A joke broke the ice – we pretended that Mrs Whyte and the old Colonel in the play had something going between them. We improvised backstage and had a mock quarrel, which we carried on into the street afterwards, with Wendy shouting from a taxi, to the astonishment of passers-by, 'You'll hear from my solicitor in the morning!' "

When I asked Frances how she prepares for a part she said, "Early on I formulated my own Stanislavsky method—it breaks down a part into various components. One of the rules is that you analyse a character, first deciding what are its attractive features. Then, on the other side, you must find the negative qualities. Even in the most perfect heroine you must *try* to find certain faults, otherwise it is not a rounded character and nobody is going to believe it."

Frances is convinced that ". . . you've got to like the characters you portray, even tiresome or unpleasant ones, otherwise you can't play them, because all people like themselves. You have to find something that justifies their behaviour to themselves, even if to nobody else."

This empathy, this warmth in Frances's acting and personality communicates itself to the audience. As Kenneth Tynan wrote of her performance in *A Taste of Honey*, "This is an actress with a lot of love to give."

Joan Littlewood, London, 1965

Joan Littlewood

Of all my theatrical experiences the happiest was my association in London in late 1955 with the inspiring and idiosyncratic Joan Littlewood and the Theatre Workshop Company at the Theatre Royal, Stratford East.

The West End stage in the early 1950s was characterized by excellent acting, polished productions, stylish revivals of the classics, lightweight comedies and musicals, and a sprinkling of semi-serious but unchallenging 'straight' plays. The more 'advanced' theatre was represented by the verse dramas of T. S. Eliot and Christopher Fry, and by Fry's translations of Anouilh and Giraudoux. Theatre clubs offered more unusual fare, and small left-wing groups performed 'social-realist' plays to very limited audiences.

My first experience of an altogether different type of British theatre was a performance in May 1952 at the Embassy, Swiss Cottage, of *Uranium 235* by folk-singer Ewan McColl. This play, originally written in 1945, shortly after the atom bomb was dropped on Hiroshima, covers the entire history of atomic energy. The company of twelve who played the 57 characters was founded and directed by an extraordinary woman who was soon to become something of a legend – Joan Littlewood.

Uranium 235 may have lacked the smooth professionalism of the West End—Joan's productions were never without their rough edges—but this was more than made up for by the vitality and versatility of the actors, the expressive dance-mime sequences, the imaginative staging on a limited budget, and by the topicality of the play itself. Without heavy didacticism or social-realist literalism, but with fantasy and satiric humour, it dramatized the splitting of the atom and its awesome consequences.

The robust Littlewood touch was equally evident in her 1954 production of *The Good Soldier Schweik*, skilfully adapted from the Czech writer Jaroslav Hašek's satirical anti-war novel. The sets and costumes were entirely in black and white in the style of Josef Lada's blunt, semi-naive illustrations to the book. George Cooper in the title role looked astonishingly like the 'simple-sly' character in the drawing, but as in *Uranium 235* it was the work of the whole company rather than one star performance that was impressive. *Schweik* was both funny and moving and as a total experience it was, I felt, what theatre should be and so rarely is.

When a friend suggested in the autumn of 1955 that I contact Joan Littlewood, I did so without delay. I had had plenty of experience designing for repertory and had done sets for two plays in the West End but I knew that Theatre Workshop was what I wanted, even though it was hardly the road to riches.

I did not meet Joan right away. My appointment was with John Bury, Theatre Workshop's regular designer, carpenter and stage manager. From the Stratford underground station in the East End I walked with my portfolio through the dingy streets of terraced houses to the Theatre Royal in Angel Lane. It was Joan's ambition to build up a working-class audience in the community, such as the company had sometimes encountered on tour in Wales and the North of England. Even though this was never really achieved, the theatre's location in an unfashionable and poor neighbourhood gave it a unique character, very different from Shaftesbury Avenue.

The Theatre Royal, in a run-down state when the company took it over in 1953, was still shabby, draughty and uncomfortable, but it had preserved something of the atmosphere of the Victorian playhouse and Palace of Varieties that it once had been. There was an exhilarating sense of 'work in progress'.

John Bury, tall and amiable, looked at my work. He said that he would suggest to Joan that I do the sets and costumes for the

Christmas production of Eugène Labiche's mid-19th-century comedy *An Italian Straw Hat*.

Soon afterwards I met Joan and her close friend and General Manager, Gerry Raffles. With his dark curly hair he looked like a taller, neater and smoother Brendan Behan. Gerry had performed miracles in raising enough money to keep the theatre going, an often thankless task. I felt immediately at home in the informal yet concentrated atmosphere.

Joan was then just past forty, small and solidly built, full of energy and ideas. She chain-smoked Gauloises and always wore the little woollen hat at the back of her head that has become her own special trademark. An engaging scruffiness was combined with real style. Her face, with the drooping eyelids and peasant-like features, was usually puckered in thought as she wrestled with a problem or sorted out her ideas, but it would light up now and then in a mischievous grin.

Basically serious, Joan also has a raffish, Rabelaisian side that surfaces from time to time. I had heard how, at seventeen, after leaving the Royal Academy of Dramatic Art in London, which came to represent much of what she detested in 'establishment' theatre, she had walked and hitch-hiked her way to Manchester, where in 1933 she founded the Theatre of Action. It was easy to imagine her taking to the road again should the need arise.

We began to discuss the sets for *An Italian Straw Hat*. René Clair, in his silent film *Un chapeau de paille d'Italie*, had dressed his characters in the costumes of the 1890s, giving them a Douanier Rousseau look. We agreed to set the play in 1851, when it had been written. I envisaged sets that would evoke, without duplicating, the Paris 'vaudeville' theatre of the mid-19th century, in which light comedies were interspersed with songs and dances. The text we used was an adaptation from the French by an American, Theodore Hoffman. I spent several days in the reading room of the British Museum, steeping myself in the French comic periodicals of the time: *Le Charivari*, *La Caricature* and *Le journal amusant*.

61

I designed reversible sets for four of the acts but left the stage open (except for a sentry-box) for the Paris square in Act V. The tall grilles suggesting park gates had large 'iron' scrolls made of thick coils of black-painted rope. Throughout the play there were permanent towers on either side representing angled exterior walls, with posters, announcements and chalk graffiti of the period. As Joan said, "The inner sets are the play, the towers are Claude's *comments* on the play." This sounds Brechtian although I knew next to nothing about Brecht at the time.

A designer inevitably has less frequent contact with the director than the actors. My relationship with Joan was extremely cordial throughout but I was aware that, although she cherished her actors – her 'nuts' as she called them—she could be extremely hard on them at times, saying such things as, "You made a right old balls-up of that scene!" Believing as she does in improvisation, she was liable to change the concept of the production at a late stage in rehearsals, to the dismay of the cast, who often had to admit in the end that she was right. However, her suggestions were usually provocative in a constructive way, reinforced by her extensive knowledge of art and theatre history. While moments of tension were inevitable, there was truly a feeling of 'family' about the company.

An Italian Straw Hat ran for three weeks and was well received. Joan then asked me to design new costumes for *Edward II*, which she was planning to take to the Paris Festival at the Théâtre Sarah-Bernhardt in the summer of 1956, along with *Schweik*. I did the sketches and she was enthusiastic but the transportation of two productions to Paris proved too costly and only *Schweik* was taken.

In the autumn of 1956 I returned to New York after six years in England. In retrospect I am glad that my association with Theatre Workshop was in 1955 for that was the last year in which the company still maintained some of its original cohesive character and style. But, as Ewan McColl had feared, the move to Stratford East had made Theatre Workshop accessible to the London critics,

Joan Littlewood, London, 1967

63

it had led to growing popularity with a non-local audience, and the transfers to the West End had involved certain compromises, dispersal of the actors and other penalties of success.

Joan was always happier in the role of rebel and underdog. Being accepted by the establishment—one newspaper article was headed 'Joan of London'—was a confusing and disorientating experience for her. But there were still memorable achievements. Brendan Behan's *The Quare Fellow* (1956) and *The Hostage* (1958) would never have been written without constant prodding from Joan and Gerry. Later came Shelagh Delaney's *A Taste of Honey* (1958), with its outstanding performances by Frances Cuka, Avis Bunnage and Murray Melvin, and Frank Norman's highly successful *Fings Ain't Wot They Used T'Be* (1960).

Financial pressures were eased but long runs and other problems led to Joan's leaving the company in 1961. She returned in 1963 to direct the brilliant and moving *Oh What a Lovely War* but that too lost some of its impact on being transferred to the West End, and suffered even more when presented on Broadway in 1964.

I saw very little of Joan in the 1960s. I read of her project, never realized, for a Fun Palace on the banks of the Thames in the East End, and heard that in 1965–66 she was working with the International Cultural Centre in Tunisia. I learned that Gerry Raffles had died suddenly in France in April 1975, and that Joan had left England early the following year to make her home there, but I had no details, and no-one seemed to know her exact whereabouts.

Joan reappeared in my life under the most surprising circumstances, in New York, in the late autumn of 1979. I had just given a lecture on art at the Metropolitan Museum and was in the auditorium office collecting my things when an oddly familiar figure walked up to me and said, "You won't remember me." I said, "You look like Joan Littlewood." She replied, "I *was* Joan Littlewood!" which gave me a very strange sensation indeed. Her face was more lined than before but she still wore a woollen cap, this one with a peak and small pom-pom, at the back of her head.

Joan Littlewood, New York, 1979

My wife arrived to collect me and we invited Joan to have a meal with us. On the way she told us what a traumatic experience Gerry's death had been. He had left no will and creditors were beleaguering their house in Blackheath. The Theatre Royal, under different management, was in jeopardy, and the company was scattered. In desperation she had left for France and had finally settled in Vienne, near to where Gerry had died of a heart attack. Since then she had led a wretched existence, 'living like a ghost' in a rented room.

Friends had become so alarmed that they had arranged for her to fly to America for medical treatment. And so it was that on that cold Saturday afternoon in November 1979 she was wandering down Fifth Avenue and saw an announcement of my lecture in the lobby of the Metropolitan Museum.

After our meal we went back to our apartment and Sue read her some of her poems while I sketched Joan for the first time since 1967. A week or so later, after visiting friends in Annapolis, Joan returned to France.

Since that meeting her circumstances have improved, and although she has never ceased to grieve, some of her old resilience has returned. I get postcards and letters from time to time, in which the handwriting, especially on the envelopes, is 'designed' in her characteristic baroque script.

Joan was present in spirit, if not in the flesh, at a lively cabaret programme held at the Theatre Royal in May 1981 to celebrate the publication of Howard Goorney's book *The Theatre Workshop Story* and the 25th anniversary of the first production of Brendan Behan's *The Quare Fellow*.

The neighbourhood had changed so completely, after massive 'redevelopment', that it was hard to find the theatre. The building was still intact, however, in better condition than formerly, and the area in front of it has been renamed 'Gerry Raffles Square'.

It was a nostalgic as well as a joyous occasion. Murray Melvin, still as slender as when he had played the art student Geoffrey in *A Taste of Honey*, had assembled at short notice as many of the original company as he could locate. Along with Avis Bunnage and Howard Goorney – the 'old lags' as they called themselves – were Brian Murphy, Frances Cuka, Maxwell Shaw and many others from the old days. Balloons hanging from the flies added to the festive atmosphere.

The programme had been thrown together at the last minute and consisted mainly of skits, excerpts and songs—from *The Quare Fellow, The Hostage, Fings Ain't Wot They Used T'Be* and *Oh What a Lovely War*. Frances Cuka sang the poignant 'Black Boy' from *A Taste of Honey*. In one solo number, Victor Spinetti, who was the M. C. in *Lovely War*, carried on an imaginary phone conversation

The 25th anniversary cabaret at the Theatre Royal, Stratford East, 24 May 1981. From left to right: Avis Bunnage, Frances Cuka (in the background), Howard Goorney and Brian Murphy.

with Joan in Vienne, and one could easily conjure up her pungent replies.

Daniel Farson wrote in the London *Sunday Telegraph* in September 1981 that Shaftesbury Avenue needed another 'Littlewood explosion', and he noted that many actors would ". . . cross the world to work with her again." Even if she never returns to the theatre she will be remembered as having revitalized the convention-ridden British stage of the 1950s, with repercussions felt for many years in other countries as well. Without her lusty, free-wheeling spirit, 'Fings Ain't Wot They Used T'Be'!

Claude
Marks
New York, May
1963.

A Breandán ó
beacáin
Brendan
Behan

Brendan Behan

In 1960 Brendan Behan's wild and joyous play *The Hostage* was being performed on Broadway by members of London's Theatre Workshop, where, under the direction of Joan Littlewood, his work had first been produced. This free-wheeling play, combining outlandish characters, colourful dialogue, and snatches of song and dance, set in a disreputable Dublin lodging-house and pub against the troubled background of the British-Irish conflict, brought a breath of fresh air to Broadway.

There was a certain amount of improvisation, especially on those evenings when the irrepressible author, in varying degrees of inebriation, would insert himself into the action, his tousled head appearing unexpectedly at a window, or popping up from behind the bar. One evening when there had been no such interruption, Avis Bunnage, playing Meg Dillon, the proprietress of the tavern, ad-libbed, "Thank goodness Brendan isn't here tonight!" Whereupon an unmistakable voice was heard from the second balcony, "I'm watching yer!"

On some evenings Brendan would appear on stage for the curtain call, singing lustily with the cast in the final chorus that began:

> Oh, there's no place on earth like the world,
> No matter wherever you be. . . .

No place in New York was like the Chelsea Hotel in the early 1960s. In the lobby or elevator one might encounter the tall, lean, serious Arthur Miller, the composer Virgil Thomson who has lived there many years, the poet Leonie Adams, the dancer Katherine Dunham, and an assortment of artists and writers, some better known than others. A plaque outside the hotel is a reminder that residents in the past have included Thomas Wolfe, the painter John Sloan, and Dylan Thomas.

I had an apartment on the tenth floor with my wife and son, and a studio on the second. One day in 1963, when taking the elevator to the lobby, I noticed among my fellow-passengers a dark-haired, rumpled figure accompanied by two friends. He looked at me with a nod of semi-recognition. I realized that this was Brendan Behan, whom I had only met once, very briefly, in the mid-1950s in London, when he had been brought to our Hampstead home by the musician John Beckett, Samuel Beckett's cousin. Brendan, not yet the celebrity and 'roaring boyo', had sat quietly and amiably in the room, and I hardly remembered his visit.

My wife Sue and our son David first experienced his more colourful side on the opening night of his play *The Quare Fellow* at Theatre Workshop, Stratford East, London in late 1956. I had already returned to the States. Brendan, leaning against the wall of the foyer, was cheerfully soused, his shirt open down to his navel, and surrounded by what my son described as 'IRA types in raincoats'. David, then twelve years old, offered Brendan some sweets from a paper bag, which Brendan grabbed, dipped into and passed around to his friends.

During the run of *The Hostage* Brendan and his wife Beatrice were our neighbours. He had been asked to leave the Algonquin Hotel—we never quite discovered the circumstances—and he had found a haven at the ever-tolerant Chelsea. In retrospect his last stay there may have been 'the beginning of the end', but we found that there was a private Brendan, warm, sensitive, thoughtful and keenly observant, especially when 'off the gargle'.

In public Brendan the performer took over; he was a wonderfully witty story-teller but too many drinks made him irrational and incoherent and sometimes ugly and aggressive. He seemed relaxed and comfortable while visiting us and, finding him a splendid

Claude
Marks
1963

subject, I made a number of drawings, never asking him to pose for very long at a time. In two of the sketches he was reading my article on Gordon Craig in *Theatre Arts*. At one point he growled, "I wish to hell someone would write about *me* like that!" He signed several of the drawings, first in Gaelic then in English. In one sketch, which he did not see, he was stretched out on the sofa, with a rather pathetic, doleful expression on his face.

One day, in the hotel lobby, he ran into our son David and a girlfriend who was wearing a white cotton dress with eyelet embroidery. Brendan took hold of a corner of the dress and shouted: "She's got me pyjamas!"

One of his favourite haunts was the Oasis (it no longer exists), a few doors from the Chelsea. He would make outrageous comments about some of the people entering the bar. Once, in a jovial mood, and with just the right amount of tipsiness, he burst into song, to the tune of *Land of Hope and Glory*:

> I'm Lady Chatterley's lover,
> A game game-keeper am I. . . .

I sketched him as he was singing. He had quite a good voice although it had turned wheezy over the years. He must have been feeling benevolent that day for at one point he made the remark, surprisingly enough for an Irish nationalist of long standing: "The British royal family—they're not such a bad lot, you know. . . ."

On other days he could grow testy; once, when asked how his brother Dominic was and what he was doing, he replied, "Who the hell cares?" One afternoon, when returning from seeing the British film directed by Joan Littlewood, *Sparrers Can't Sing*, I stopped by the Oasis. Brendan and Beatrice were in a booth. Brendan was slumped over the table, his head buried in his arms: he seemed to have passed out completely. I mentioned to Beatrice that I had just seen this entertaining film dealing with London low life. I heard a rumble from the corner, and Brendan's muffled voice emerged, "A fat lot you know about low life!"

My last memory of Brendan was a quick glimpse of him sitting in the Oasis. My wife and I were leaving for Italy and by the time we returned to New York there had been a real deterioration. His last hectic days, and his death in Ireland in May 1964, have been fully described elsewhere.

In 1969 I had the rare pleasure of being shown round Dublin by that gentle and revered Irish-American poet and man of letters, Padraic Colum, then aged 89. He recalled an incident following the successful Dublin opening of *The Quare Fellow* in 1954. Crossing O'Connell Bridge he saw Brendan and two of his cronies staggering towards him; they had obviously been on an extensive pub crawl. As Padraic was passing the rowdy trio he turned and said, "I enjoyed your play, Brendan." Brendan, decidedly not in the mood for compliments, lurched around and glared bleary-eyed at Padraic.

73

In his thick brogue he blurted out, "Well, it's a hell of a lot better than *yoor* bloody plays!" Padraic was still able to laugh at this typical Behanism and declared that it was impossible to take offence.

The painter Raphael Soyer has called him "the tragic and lovable Brendan Behan" and indeed, impossible though he was at times, and ultimately self-destructive, my family and I have warm and affectionate memories of him. His colourful personality made such an impression that I made two conté crayon drawings of him from memory. The profile view suggests one of the fleshier Roman emperors, perhaps Vespasian, stamped on a coin. The other drawing, acquired by a collector in Oxford, England, evokes the rollicking, Bacchanalian Brendan, with a roguish smile and a pudgy hand grasping a glass.

Behan's autobiographical *Borstal Boy*, and his plays *The Quare Fellow* and *The Hostage*, have contributed to the rich gallery of Irish eccentrics. His last work, *Richard's Cork Leg*, was destined to remain a fragment. But, as with that very different literary personality, Dr Samuel Johnson, it may well be that Brendan Behan's most memorable creation was Brendan himself.

All of the drawings in this chapter were done in the artist's studio at the Chelsea Hotel, New York, in 1963.

Breandán
Ó Beacáin

Brendan
Behan

Clarke
Marks
New York, May, 1963

75

Alec Guinness as Dylan Thomas in Dylan,
at the Plymouth Theatre, New York, 1964.

Alec Guinness

Until 1963, when I saw him play Dylan Thomas on Broadway, Alec Guinness was known to me solely through his movie roles, among them the appealing Herbert Pocket in *Great Expectations*, the sinister Fagin in *Oliver Twist*, the debonair bigamist in *The Captain's Paradise*, the array of aristocratic and rapidly disposed-of D'Ascoynes in *Kind Hearts and Coronets* and, of course, his stoical, obdurate British officer in *The Bridge on the River Kwai*.

Dylan gave me my first opportunity to admire his stage performance although, as I later discovered, he had doubled as Osric and the Third Player in John Gielgud's great production of *Hamlet* at the New Theatre in London, which I had seen many years before.

Guinness showed his amazing versatility in *Dylan* for nothing could have been further from his own reticent outward personality than the rowdy and reckless Welsh poet, whose alcoholism had brought on his death in 1953 during his third tour of the United States. Having met Dylan Thomas in Iowa City some years before, and heard his superb reading of his own and other poems, I was struck by the extent to which Guinness conveyed the inspired poet, the warm, robust, yet finally pathetic human being, and the pudgy, gone-to-seed cherub. Guinness paid several visits to the White Horse Tavern, Dylan's favourite bar in Greenwich Village, in preparing for the role.

After the performance I knocked on Guinness's dressing-room door and showed him some photostats of my drawings, including one of John Gielgud. "That's very good of John," he remarked. He asked whether I wanted to draw him as himself or as Dylan. I said,

"As yourself." "How long will that take?" "Oh, about twenty minutes"—something of an underestimate! I then said, "Of course, it would be most interesting to draw you as Dylan as well." He glanced at his watch: "That would be forty minutes." Not wishing to tire him in view of his strenuous role, I gladly settled for sketching him as his elusive self, realizing that that would be the greater challenge. We agreed on a time, between a matinée and evening performance.

When I arrived for the sitting, he was courteous, obliging, shy, and a little remote. I noticed on the wall beside his dressing-table a postcard reproduction of one of Giotto's religious frescoes in Padua. Guinness had been converted to Catholicism some time before, and I realized that there was a priestly air about him that could provide a clue to my approach.

After he had settled in his chair by the dressing-table, this extraordinary actor, who could transform himself into so many different characters, seemed uncertain what to do when posing as himself. Slowly, haltingly, he crossed his arms over his chest, which again suggested some dedicated, contemplative monk. Meanwhile he gazed vaguely into space with a bland expression in which there was the merest hint of a smile—some hidden mischief, a puckishness beneath the apparent serenity. I felt that it was important to suggest the potentiality of many different roles; here was a neutral instrument which, given the right stimulus, could produce any number of fascinating melodies.

Guinness posed impeccably, without stirring. I was glad to see that in the finished drawing there was a touch of humour around the eyes, and the faintest suggestion of an enigmatic smile. The sparse wisps of hair on the top of his head created a kind of aura, which seemed entirely appropriate. He was apparently pleased with the result and I felt that the session was a success.

Several days later I sent him a photostat of the drawing and I received an answer in his tiny, neat handwriting. He thanked me, and added, "I find it flattering, but I am not averse to that."

Alec Guinness, New York, 1964.

*Laurence Olivier as Othello, at the
Chichester Festival Theatre, 1964.*

80

Laurence Olivier

To say that Laurence Olivier is 'on' for much of the time in no way implies a lack of sincerity. From several meetings with him I have invariably come away with a feeling of his warmth, courtesy and genuine responsiveness. Yet the mood on each occasion has been different, with a touch of the unexpected, and enlivened at times by his mischievous humour. Olivier's complexity is part of his fascination; the various 'personae' he tends to assume offstage are perhaps 'daytime' manifestations of that vital energy, imagination and contained power that make his performances so compelling.

My first opportunity to meet Olivier came in New York in January 1961, in connection with a ceremony I was helping to organize at the Neighborhood Playhouse to celebrate Gordon Craig's 89th birthday. Craig, as the 'grand-daddy' of modern stage design, was to be made an honorary member of the United Scenic Artists' Union.

Since Olivier was then starring in Anouilh's *Becket* at the St. James's Theatre on Broadway, he was the obvious choice to accept the specially designed plaque on behalf of Craig, who was unable to make the journey himself from his home in France. In spite of his busy schedule and personal preoccupations, Olivier agreed, in honour of 'the master', to take part in the ceremony.

I was delegated to call on him backstage on a matinée day, between shows, to discuss the programme. Olivier was in his dressing-room, having shed most of his Becket costume, and was removing his make-up. He was affable but a bit tense, and obviously had much on his mind. On seeing the list of planned speeches he exclaimed, "Christ, when do I eat?" His point was well taken, for the ceremony was scheduled for mid-afternoon and the sequence of speakers made it seem dangerously drawn out.

Olivier suggested ways of condensing the programme and then added, "You've got to watch some of these people—this'll be their *big moment!*" I promised that we would try to keep the time element under control and he said, "I know what these things can be like." Then, after a pause, he added, "Look—I'm doing this for Craig and I'm doing it for *you.*" By 'you' I realized that he meant the Union, and I thanked him on their behalf.

When he appeared at the Neighborhood Playhouse on the afternoon of the event, he had his low-key, seemingly self-effacing 'assistant bank manager' look, and yet one was thoroughly aware of his presence. After viewing the small Craig exhibition in the lobby, he said, almost plaintively, "Mr Marks, could we *please* begin?" and we all proceeded to the platform. The speeches and excerpts were kept mercifully brief, with the exception of Etienne Decroux, whose slow, declamatory French had to be translated, sentence by sentence. As he was speaking, one could see Olivier trying hard to control his impatience.

Within the next few days most of the participants had signed the presentation plaque but it still lacked Olivier's signature. It was decided that I should call once more at the theatre, to thank Olivier for his cooperation and to ask him to sign.

This time he was in a delightful mood and greeted me cordially. As I sat by his dressing-table he asked if I would like a drink and poured me a scotch. "Will you join me, Sir Laurence?" I asked, and he replied, with a conspiratorial 'mischievous schoolboy' expression on his face: "No, I'm being a good boy now!" I had the feeling that things were looking brighter for him generally.

We agreed that the Craig ceremony had gone quite smoothly, but then he asked, "Who was that *bloody* old Frenchman?" He puffed out his chest and gave a hilarious imitation of Decroux's voice and manner. "That was Etienne Decroux, who taught mime

Laurence Olivier as Edgar in the National Theatre's production of
Strindberg's The Dance of Death, *at the Old Vic, London, 1967.*

To the Artist
all wishes
& thanks

Claude
Marks
1972

Laurence Olivier as James Tyrone in the National Theatre's production of Long Day's Journey into Night *by Eugene O'Neill, at the New Theatre, London, 1972.*

to Jean-Louis Barrault," I replied. "Oh," exclaimed Olivier, "so it was *he* who taught Barrault to do that stuff! When Barrault brought his company to the St. James's Theatre [in 1956, when that London theatre was managed by Olivier and Vivien Leigh] I told him, '*Don't do that in my theatre*'—and he *did!*"

When I said that we would like to have his signature on the plaque to send to Craig, I added, "He admires you very much." "Oh, does he?" said Olivier. "Well then, I'll jolly well sign in the middle!" which he proceeded to do, in his bold, self-assured handwriting.

The first time I actually drew Olivier was in 1964, during his performance as Othello at the Chichester Festival Theatre. Although I was not at all happy with his interpretation of the Moor, there were some gripping moments, and I felt that a couple of my action sketches, one of which I asked him to sign, were successful.

My favourite drawings of Olivier, however, were done at a matinée of Strindberg's *The Dance of Death* at the National Theatre (at the Old Vic) in 1967. The sardonic humour and savage frustration of his Edgar made it, to my mind, one of his most brilliant creations.

In 1972, on my last evening in London before returning to New York, I saw Olivier's engrossing, multi-layered performance as James Tyrone in a splendid National Theatre production of Eugene O'Neill's *Long Day's Journey into Night*. Considering Olivier's usual fondness for elaborate make-up, putty noses and so on, it was remarkable how, without any external devices, he achieved an astonishing physical resemblance to later photographs of Eugene's father, James O'Neill, as well as conveying the Irish-American background and the conflicts and tensions within the character.

Visiting Olivier backstage afterwards, I showed him sketches made during the performance as well as some that he had not seen of *The Dance of Death*. He was most complimentary and inscribed one of the drawings: "To the artist, all wishes and thanks." Looking at one of the sketches of Edgar he remarked, "That was child's play

Laurence Olivier as Shylock in the National Theatre's production of The Merchant of Venice, *at the Old Vic, London, 1974.*

compared to this", meaning James Tyrone. I remarked on how successful his performance and the entire production had been in bringing out whatever humour could be found in O'Neill. "Wait a minute," he said, "I want to show you something." He fetched a photograph from an adjoining room and said, "This was given me a few evenings ago by Oona O'Neill—Mrs Chaplin." It showed a

Laurence Olivier, New York, 1980.

youngish, handsome Eugene O'Neill posing in a bathing suit, not outdoors but in a living-room. He was facing the camera with his arms upraised as if about to dive. Olivier said with a chuckle, "Vain old boy, wasn't he?" As I left he wished me *bon voyage*.

On a previous occasion I had asked Olivier if he would pose for me 'as himself', but he was obviously reluctant and I did not pursue the matter. Great actor that he is, his most vivid qualities are revealed in his stage roles and, with his leonine features, he is an ideal subject for action sketches during performance.

Only once, in 1980, when he and Joan Plowright appeared on a television interview with Dick Cavett, did I have the opportunity to attempt a 'straight' portrait. Seeing the Oliviers together one was aware of a warm, happy partnership. His own comments were quiet, relaxed and thoughtful. There was no role-playing yet there was always that elusive, mysterious quality in the eyes that I tried to suggest in my sketch.

One of my favourite stories about 'Sir' illustrates his irrepressible humour. A young actor was about to tackle the role of Oedipus. This was a part that Olivier, in a famous double bill in 1945, had played on the same evening as Mr Puff in Sheridan's *The Critic*. The actor asked him how he had achieved that overwhelming, almost animal cry of sheer agony and horror on discovering the fatal secret. Olivier replied, "It's simple, dear boy. Just follow the text. It says, 'Oh! Oh! Oh!' "

Vanessa Redgrave

Vanessa Redgrave once described herself and her extraordinary family as 'the sprigs of a great and beautiful tree'. The Redgrave family tree is indeed impressive, and rooted for several generations in the theatre. Her parents, Sir Michael Redgrave and Rachel Kempson, are illustrious figures on the British stage, her grandfather and grandmother were both well-known actors, and a great-grandfather with the resounding name of Fortunatus Augustus was the hero of countless Victorian melodramas.

The tree simile is particularly appropriate for Vanessa, who, nearly six feet tall and with red-gold hair, could be compared to a poplar in the early autumn. But one London critic, enchanted by her now legendary Rosalind in *As You Like It* at the Aldwych Theatre in 1961, compared the young Vanessa to 'a sexy giraffe'! Even those who resent her political activism admire her magnetism and sensitivity as an actress, enhanced by her spectacular beauty.

Michael Elliott, who directed Vanessa in a production of Ibsen's *The Lady from the Sea* at the Circle in the Square, Off-Broadway in New York in 1976, said of her, "Politically, she's leading such a strange life, but she never lets politics interfere with her acting". In her actual performance, whether as the eccentric Miss Jean Brodie on the stage, or as the errant, love-struck Guinevere in the film *Camelot*, there is no hint of her militant radicalism. However, once, after rehearsing a passionate scene in *Antony and Cleopatra* she was known to call an Equity meeting, which certainly broke the magic spell! She herself has said, "Actors are probably prone to schizophrenia", but according to Michael Elliott, Vanessa is schizophrenic

Vanessa Redgrave as Miss Brodie in The Prime of Miss
Jean Brodie *(adapted from Muriel Spark's novel by Jay
Preston Allen), at Wyndham's Theatre, London, 1966.*

Claude Marks
1966

"I'm Miss Jean Brodie, and I'm in my prime!"

'in a wonderful way'. If there is a link between the two contrasting aspects of her life, it is that rare quality of 'blinding sincerity'.

My first view of Vanessa on stage was at Wyndham's Theatre in London in the summer of 1966 when she gave an unforgettable performance in *The Prime of Miss Jean Brodie*, adapted by Jay Preston Allen from the novel by Muriel Spark. As the Edinburgh school-teacher with 'advanced' but dangerously wrongheaded views imposed on her impressionable pupils—*la crème de la crème*—she was a fascinating mixture of provincial Pre-Raphaelitism (with a Scottish accent), florid self-dramatization, and an odd, angular quirkiness.

She was wonderful to sketch, with her reddish hair in a tight but 'artistic' bun, her long string of beads, and her flowing, slightly *passé* clothes. She used her arms and hands beautifully, applying hand-lotion from a bottle at strategic moments—to the great annoyance of the headmistress, with whom she was having a tense interview.

I sent Vanessa a group of photostats of the sketches, and asked if she would pose for me as Miss Brodie. She wrote back on notepaper headed Vanessa Richardson (she was at that time married to the director Tony Richardson), that she was "thrilled to get the drawings", and that she particularly liked the full-length one of 'potty Brodie' seated, during her confrontation with the headmistress. She explained that in addition to playing every evening, she was filming during the day, and taking dancing lessons in preparation for the movie *Isadora*, but that at some future time she would be happy to pose.

My opportunity came ten years later in New York when she played Ellida in Ibsen's *The Lady from the Sea*. She had played the other female role in the play, Boletta, six years before in London; for that performance, as well as for her Kate in *The Taming of the Shrew*, she had received the London *Evening Standard's* 1961 award as the best actress of the year. (The award was repeated in 1967, the year she played Ellida in New York.)

The production at the Circle in the Square was hampered by the presentation in the round, and the cast was uneven. It was Vanessa, projecting both the human dilemma and transcendental yearning of the character, who provided the enchantment. After one matinée there was a session with the audience in which Vanessa and other members of the company discussed the play. She answered questions in a friendly, spontaneous and informative manner, and stressed the modernity of Ibsen. She said on another occasion, "I think more highly of Ibsen than I do of Chekhov".

Vanessa posed for me twice in costume, and was most cooperative, even sprinkling water on her hair to give it the 'Lady from the Sea' look. My first drawing was rather stiff, but returning on another evening I came close to capturing the combination of classical dignity and feminine warmth that she conveyed in the part.

Vanessa Redgrave as Ellida in Ibsen's The Lady from the Sea, *at the Circle in the Square, New York, 1976: water colour and pen and ink.*

Appropriately, she signed the first drawing "Vanessa Redgrave" and the second drawing "Vanessa". At one point the phone rang and I was amused when she answered, "I can't talk now. I'm posing for Claude Marks"!

At the end of our first session, she prepared to hurry to her apartment to be with her little son Carlo (by the Italian actor Franco Nero). After I had finished the second drawing, she announced that it was time for her to leave for a meeting of the Workers' Revolutionary Party, a Trotskyite organization in which her brother Corin is also active. She changed hurriedly, and I accompanied her into the noisy midtown street. I am a fast walker, but as she strode purposefully toward Eighth Avenue, where we said goodbye, I had difficulty keeping up with her! Yet tall and long-limbed as she is, she is never awkward or ungraceful.

There is no 'stardom' about Vanessa. She will stand in the rain in London outside theatre stage doors and job centres, handing out Workers' Revolutionary Party pamphlets and newspapers, and arguing politics. She has never shied away from controversy.

There were some who, because of her outspoken support for the Palestine Liberation Organization, violently protested at her being cast in the leading role of Fania Fénélon (the Jewish survivor of the Nazi concentration camp at Auschwitz) in the American TV production of *Playing for Time* in September 1980, but they could not deny that she gave a ". . . powerful, subtle and compassionate performance", to quote the *Newsweek* critic, Jack Kroll.

An actress friend of mine, returning to London after a long absence, knew that she was home again when she walked into an Equity meeting and heard the chairman exclaim, "Will you please sit *down*, Vanessa!" And there was Vanessa, her grey eyes flashing, waving her arms, in the midst of an impassioned speech! If she is often a storm centre, there is also sunshine and warmth in her personality, and a special radiance in her acting. Her sister Lynn once said, "I love her a lot. I think she's a great actress. I'm a raging capitalist. . . . She's one of the great eccentrics."

Glenda Jackson

Although she has portrayed Queen Elizabeth I, and played many period and classical roles with conviction and authority, Glenda Jackson is very much a woman of today. Thoroughly professional in her work, she combines in her offstage personality a matter-of-fact, down-to-earth approach to life (part of her North of England background) with a keen, questioning intelligence and a warm but unsentimental feeling for people.

Glenda Jackson is essentially a private person and at times her reserve, or rather her habitual 'down-playing' of her emotions, has been mistaken for aloofness. But to those she likes and trusts she is a loyal friend, candid and unprententious and often displaying a delightful and somewhat ironic sense of humour.

With her strong, sensitive, slightly Oriental features, she is a wonderful subject for drawing and painting. My first meeting with her was in London in 1964. She was at that time relatively unknown but after I had seen her as the narcoleptic inmate of Charenton who enacts Charlotte Corday in *Marat-Sade* I realized at once that this was someone with extraordinary qualities.

It was Peter Brook's brilliant production of Peter Weiss's play, presented by the Royal Shakespeare Company at the Aldwych Theatre, and I sketched Glenda as she stood downstage, dazed and vulnerable, in a pose of catatonic stupor and rigidity.

My wife, son and I called on Glenda after the show; she was most friendly, liked the sketch, and agreed to pose for a more detailed drawing as Corday. However, this had to be postponed as she was suddenly called to Stratford-on-Avon.

Glenda Jackson as Charlotte Corday in Peter Brook's production of
Marat-Sade *by Peter Weiss, at the Aldwych Theatre, London, 1964.*

Fortunately, in late December 1965, the Royal Shakespeare Company brought *Marat-Sade* to Broadway, where it ran for over eighteen weeks at the Martin Beck Theatre. In addition to performance sketches – Peter Brook's grouping of the 'inmates' had a sculptural as well as a choreographic quality – I drew several members of the cast who sat for me in costume. Glenda posed as Charlotte Corday in her ribboned hat and Empire blouse with the same concentration and intensity that she brought to her stage role.

Since she was to be in New York for some weeks Glenda had time to pose for a portrait in oil in my studio on Central Park West. In those days she wore her hair shoulder length and she dressed mostly in black, with just an occasional touch of colour. This, together with her pale complexion, gave her a clear-cut, positive look, not exactly severe, but certainly not 'rococo'.

In posing her I was struck by the contrast between her slight build and her powerful arms and hands. Ian Richardson, who as Marat was being stabbed nightly in his bath by Corday, said later, "When you see that North Country lass standing over you with a dagger you *know* she's got strong arms."

Glenda came a number of times to pose. The final portrait, done mostly with a palette knife, is now in a private collection in New York, but Glenda bought a large study for the painting, in brush and India ink with a touch of pastel, on brown wrapping paper, to give to her husband Roy as an anniversary present. Her comment was, "It's a good shape." When I asked her some years later how she liked having her portrait and other sketches I had made of her decorating the walls of her home, she replied with typical understatement, "They're just objects."

In the rest periods between posing Glenda spoke of her admiration for Jerzy Grotowski's starkly experimental Polish Laboratory Theatre. And she recalled with amusement her appearance as Ophelia in Stratford-on-Avon in August 1965. Penelope Gilliatt had written in her review that this was the only Ophelia she had seen who should have been playing Hamlet. Another critic had remarked that the production should have been billed as *Ophelia*. Of Shakespeare's characters Glenda said, "They're really myths. Shakespeare gives you the outlines, it's up to the actor to fill them in."

Shortly afterwards Sue and I met Glenda's husband, Roy Hodges. He was pleased with the portrait study and said that it had the watchful attentive expression that he had often seen in her during rehearsals.

We gave a party for the cast of *Marat-Sade*. Not all were able to come but it was a lively occasion. Some of our friends who had been fascinated by the play had difficulty in relating the fragile, psychopathic Corday they had seen on stage with the forthright, assertive, real-life Glenda Jackson.

Corday was the first role that had won her critical and public acclaim, first in London and now in New York. In newspaper and television interviews she was always interesting and articulate but very tense. This was largely due to the play and production which, in recreating the highly charged atmosphere of an early 19th-century insane asylum, imposed a continuous strain on the actors. It was this harrowing experience that accounted for Glenda's much misunderstood statement to Rex Reed in a *New York Times* interview: "I loathe and detest everything about the production. . . . We all loathe it. . . . It's a play that breeds sickness, with no release for the tension."

Over the years Glenda has appeared on many television talk shows and interviews in England and America. Her public 'persona' is considerably more relaxed than in those early days of celebrity and she now handles even banal questions with patience and good humour.

In 1969 we received a card from Roy and Glenda announcing the birth of their son Daniel (Danny). Glenda had added the words—"Very happy!" Roy, a fellow graduate of the Royal Academy of Dramatic Art, had worked in the theatre as an actor and director. However, he was now running an art gallery called 'The Room' in Greenwich, not far from their home in Blackheath. He invited me to exhibit my theatre drawings in his gallery in September 1970.

While preparing for the show we visited the Hodges several times. Their home could be described as 'typically suburban' were it not for the very personal taste in furniture and pictures. Glenda had recently won several awards (including two in the U.S.) for her performance as Gudrun in the film *Women in Love* and an Oscar was to follow in April 1971. She was currently working on the

Glenda Jackson as Charlotte Corday at
the Martin Beck Theatre, New York, 1966.

Glenda Jackson, New York, 1966.

Glenda Jackson, New York, 1966: oil on canvas.

101

Glenda Jackson as Elizabeth I in the BBC television series Elizabeth R,
1971. Clever use of make-up accounts for the straightened nose.

television series *Elizabeth R.* In spite of her success she has never
allowed her personal, everyday life to be affected by the 'star'
syndrome, which she views with cool objectivity.

The large pastel and ink study for Glenda's portrait was bor-
rowed for the exhibition. The London *Evening Standard* published
a photograph of Glenda, Roy and myself looking at the picture and
the accompanying article was headed: 'Knocking the legend of the
steely-hearted Glenda.' The writer saw in the portrait something of
". . . the public Glenda Jackson, serious and slightly fearsome" but

added that after talking with her for a few minutes a ". . . home-loving and—dare one say it—cosy Glenda Jackson starts appearing."

Having had her fill of playing high-strung neurotic ladies, culminating in Tchaikovsky's wife in the film *The Music Lovers* in 1971, Glenda wisely rejected the role of the hysterical hunchbacked nun in another Ken Russell movie, *The Devils*. "No more slobbering idiots for me!" she said. The film *Sunday, Bloody Sunday* was a welcome change of pace, and she subsequently displayed her flair for comedy in the movie *A Touch of Class*, which won her a second Oscar.

Whenever my wife and I were in London we would always try to arrange to meet Glenda for a meal and we enjoyed occasional reunions in New York. Given her busy schedule it was not possible to see her very often but we always felt her to be a true friend.

While she was appearing in Webster's *The White Devil* in a short season at the Old Vic in 1976, Joseph Papp asked Glenda if she would play Hamlet for him in New York. It seemed that Penelope Gilliatt's comment eleven years earlier was indeed prophetic. But although Glenda was intrigued by the idea she turned it down as she did not want to be away from London and Danny for any length of time.

However, she did return to Broadway in 1981 to play the title role in Andrew Davies's *Rose*. The role of a Midlands schoolteacher was an interesting one that gave her the opportunity to talk directly to the audience while remaining in character, creating an easy and intimate relationship that added a new dimension to her stage personality. (This device was used later to even greater effect when Glenda played the poet Stevie Smith in the film *Stevie*.)

Since *Rose* was to have only a limited run on Broadway and I had planned to leave for England within a few days, I decided that it would be a good time to do a new portrait of Glenda, to be included in an exhibition planned for the following spring in London.

Glenda posed in her dressing-room in the theatre, wearing jeans and a blue denim shirt. She had her hair very short, in a boyish cut, which gave her a sprightly, youthful appearance and emphasized her distinctive bone structure. Although animated in conversation, her face in repose tends to look serious and intent. Having caught that expression in earlier portraits I wanted a lighter feeling. I said, "Pas trop sérieuse!" and, a few minutes later, "Glenda, are you chewing gum?"—which she was! She was amused and her smile gave her an almost elfin quality which I set out to capture.

My previous drawings of her had been in pen and ink. I had lately been using water colour and pen and ink combined. After laying on the washes I discovered to my horror that my Mont Blanc fountain pen was missing. I frantically searched for it. Time was precious and the 'half-hour' call before curtain time was rapidly approaching. In the meantime Glenda phoned Roy at his hotel. I searched on the floor, the dressing-table, everywhere, and all the time Glenda was reporting everything to Roy over the phone. Finally I discovered that the pen had slipped down into the bottom of the lining of my jacket. Without hesitating I took a ball-point pen and slashed the lining in order to retrieve the Mont Blanc.

The drawing was finished just in time. We were both pleased with it and Glenda said, "Oh Claude, what a pity about your jacket." I replied, "Glenda, a lining can always be replaced—but these moments are irrecoverable."

Glenda Jackson: portrait in water colour and pen and ink, New York, 1981. She was appearing in Rose *by Andrew Davies at the time.*

Claude
Marks 1967

106

Marlene Dietrich

"Adorable, impossible, brilliant, stupid, kindly, dictatorial, helpful, perverse. . . ." These were some of the contradictory adjectives with which my son David described Marlene Dietrich. He had had the marvellous opportunity of observing her at close range while working as her lighting technician during her tour of England in 1967.

She was of course the consummate professional, whose solo performance was calculated down to the smallest detail. However, if she was bored with the audience or feeling restless she was capable of rushing through her numbers at double speed, to the despair of the conductor and musicians.

David remembers one occasion when she visited a large department store in the South Coast resort where she was appearing. She insisted that all other customers leave the store so that she could make her purchases undisturbed. The poor manager, overwhelmed by the honour of her visit, breathlessly cleared the store. Marlene whisked in, and winked at David as if to say, "You see how I can make them run!" The same sense of mischief, with a hint of self-mockery, added piquancy to her stage performance. It played against but at the same time reinforced the indestructible and legendary glamour.

Like many great artists Marlene always expected the very highest standards from the people working with her. At one theatre there were problems with the installation of the lights. The main spotlight had to be worked from the very top of the rear of the auditorium, and it could only be reached by way of a metal ladder

Claude
Marks.
1967

wedged into a narrow space. Marlene knew exactly how the light should be angled and poor David had to climb up and down the ladder five or six times before she was satisfied with the effect.

David ended up exhausted, perspiring and grimy. He said to her with a faint smile, "You know, Miss Dietrich, I'd really hate you but for one thing." "Oh," she said, intrigued, "And what is that?" He replied, "You're always right." With her famous husky blend of German and American intonations she said, "Yes, darling, I *know*. You see, I've been doing this for a *long, long* time."

When the tour was over she gave David a pair of cufflinks engraved with an oval design which, she said, reminded her of a spotlight.

Claude
Marks
1967

My own first view of Dietrich was in Salzburg at the Festival in the summer of 1933. She was accompanied by her daughter Maria and had with her, according to one enthusiastic observer, ". . . two males, one for formal, one for *in*formal wear." I only vaguely remember seeing her; she was wearing, if I recall, a white pants suit.

I next saw her thirty years later when I took David backstage to see John Gielgud after his opening night in *Ages of Man* at the Majestic Theatre on Broadway in 1963. Marlene and Gielgud were chatting and sipping champagne, and I pointed her out to David as we stood in the 'receiving line'. But he had been so thrilled by Sir John's performance that he could think of nothing else. "Who *cares* about Marlene Dietrich?" he said scornfully. He was then aged nineteen and little did he know that four years later he would have the awesome responsibility of lighting her show.

In October 1967 Marlene made her Broadway debut with a six-week engagement for her one-woman show at the Lunt-Fontanne Theatre. My mother offered to take my wife and me to a performance on my birthday on 13th November. I left a note for Marlene at the theatre a few days beforehand, saying that my son had spoken very warmly of her and had thoroughly enjoyed working with her. I told her that I would be coming to see the show and hoped that she could spare a few moments to see us afterwards.

To my delight I soon received in the mail an envelope containing a post-card-size glamour photograph of Marlene in her clinging silver lamé stage costume. On the back was written, "Mr Marks should come backstage" and underneath was her sweeping, imperious, practically illegible signature.

We had excellent seats at the performance, and as she stayed more or less in the same position throughout I was able to do a series of sketches, recording some of the changing expressions that varied according to the mood of each song. She uses very few gestures but makes each one count. The silhouette of the dress and the vertical sweep of the wrap enhanced an image that combined sophistication, toughness, humour, enjoyment, seductiveness and

Claude Marks
1973

111

a hint of vulnerability. She passed with ease from the jaunty Berlin-in-the-twenties brashness of *They call me naughty Lola* to a rendition of Pete Seeger's *Where have all the flowers gone?* that I found particularly moving.

After the show we headed for the stage door, where a crowd of fans had assembled. As the doorman looked out I waved the card with the Dietrich message. He beckoned to me and the crowd divided like the Red Sea as we made our way into the wings.

There, in the semi-darkness, stood Marlene waiting for us. Even at close range the magic and mystery were undiminished. After mentioning David and the English tour, I showed her the sketches and asked her if she would sign the two that I thought were most expressive of her 'persona'. She inscribed them with her characteristic flourish.

One of Marlene's best-known songs, dating from her Berlin years but still part of her repertoire, begins with the words "Johnny, wenn du Geburtstag hast. . ."—"When you have a birthday, come and spend the whole night with me and you will wish that you had a birthday every day!" I could not resist saying, "Miss Dietrich, ich hab' heute Geburtstag"—today's my birthday. Whereupon she leaned forward and offered me her left cheek to kiss. I said, "Miss Dietrich, that is the nicest birthday present I could have had!"

I added that I understood that she was returning to London and hoped that she would have time to pose for a more finished drawing on my next visit there. She replied, "Yes, we will have more time in London"—an intriguing remark indeed. Sadly that meeting never took place but I still have the sketches (or some of them as three are now in private collections) and I still recall the sensation of that fabulous left cheekbone!

With the exception of the final portrait, which dates from 1973, all of the drawings in this chapter were done during the performance of Marlene Dietrich's one-woman show at the Lunt-Fontanne Theatre, New York, 1967.

Leslie French

It is altogether fitting that Leslie French should have played both Ariel and Puck in his youth for even today, in his seventies, he has an ethereal, sprite-like quality. As actor, singer and director, with the added advantage of a dancer's training, he is truly an *homme de théâtre*.

I met Leslie under the pleasantest possible circumstances, in the summer of 1981. I was visiting some friends of long standing, Lewis and Betty Shaw, who live in the picturesque Italian village of Manarola on the Ligurian coast. They were eager for me to meet their old friend Leslie, who was staying nearby at Levanto.

Leslie arrived at the 'cocktail hour'. I was immediately struck by his small stature, agile movements and sensitive, bird-like features. Above all I was impressed by his penetrating yet gentle and compassionate eyes. I felt an instant rapport. With his remarkable intuition he 'sensed' several things that had recently occurred in my life. His hands, according to the Shaws, have the 'healing touch', a faculty which may come or go without warning.

I realized that I had seen him on stage on Broadway as long ago as 1938, in a charming musical play *The Two Bouquets* by Herbert and Eleanor Farjeon. Leslie had played the debonair and flirtatious Edward Gill, a part specially written for him. I vividly remember his pose in the final tableau: in a striped blazer, balanced on one leg, holding a bow and arrow—like the statue of Eros in Piccadilly Circus.

As I sketched him that afternoon, Leslie reminisced about his early career. He had first appeared on the London stage in 1914 at the age of ten, in one of Jean Sterling Mackinlay's Christmas matinées at the Little Theatre. Gordon Craig's son Teddy, who had also appeared in these shows, took Leslie to meet his grandmother, Ellen Terry, in 1916. She told Leslie that he should concentrate on being an actor. "I needed very little persuasion," said Leslie. "It was my parents who had to be won over. I remember that she wrote on the inside of my make-up box, 'Whatever you are, be that', with a few more lines, and finishing up with, 'A happy jolly New Year to Leslie French and all good wishes from Ellen Terry. Dec. 1916.' I still treasure that make-up box."

Leslie joined the Ben Greet company in 1918. He stayed for about five years, playing a variety of roles at the Comedy Theatre. Of Ben Greet he said, "He was a hard taskmaster but a generous and lovable old man. With his shock of white hair and his amazingly blue eyes and his formal clothes he looked more like an archbishop than an actor."

Encouraged by those illustrious figures, Isadora Duncan and Karsavina, Leslie took up dancing seriously in the early 1920s. "I never intended to be a dancer, it was thrust upon me; but it did help me tremendously with my work as an actor. Without the dance I would never have played Puck and Ariel. I was never with the Russian Ballet as a dancer but I did arrange dances for several London productions in the '20s and '30s."

Leslie's debut as a painter came in an equally unexpected way, as a result of meeting the sculptor Eric Gill. "I met Eric Gill in 1931—he came to see *The Tempest* at the Old Vic. John Gielgud was playing Prospero, Ralph Richardson was Caliban and I was Ariel. Gill wanted me to pose for his sculpture of Ariel for the BBC. Gielgud was unable to pose for Prospero as he had other commitments so I ended up as the model for both figures.

"During one of these sessions Eric Gill said to me, 'The only pictures to have in your house are the very best or ones that you have painted yourself.' I said, 'But I can't paint.' 'Yes you can, everyone can. Here, take this charcoal and draw me.' He posed

Leslie French, Manarola, Italy, 1981.

and I drew. We laughed a lot, but the result was that I eventually had an exhibition in London and to my astonishment sold twelve canvasses."

In 1956 Leslie was invited to South Africa to direct *The Taming of the Shrew* at the Maynardville Open Air Theatre in Cape Town. He only consented on the condition that it played to multi-racial audiences, and this policy has been observed there ever since. He regards it as ". . . the finest open-air theatre in the world" and in 1964 a season of Shakespeare plays was presented there as part of a triple celebration – the theatre's tenth anniversary, Leslie's fifty years as an actor, and the 400th anniversary of Shakespeare's birth!

I was very pleased with my drawing of Leslie and it remains one of my favourites as it captures, I believe, something of his candour and sensitivity. As we accompanied him down the hill to the little railway station by the sea to catch his train back to Levanto, Leslie told us about his part in the film *Death in Venice*. As the hotel clerk he had only one scene with Dirk Bogarde, who had played it entirely with his back to the camera so as not to detract from Leslie's performance. Leslie was very touched by this generosity and it indicates the high regard in which he is held by his colleagues. He is not only a dedicated and versatile artist, but a rare and ever-youthful spirit.

Paul Rogers

Considered one of Britain's outstanding actors, Paul Rogers is a warm, vital and highly articulate man—a strong, engaging personality offstage as well as on. The variety of his roles in both classical and modern plays is astonishing. He approaches each part with freshness and enthusiasm and even when tackling a well-known play he explores it as if it had never been done before.

In a recent conversation with me Paul said that he envied Richard Burbage, the original interpreter of Shakespeare's Hamlet, Lear, Othello, Richard III and Antony. Of him and the other actors of his day at the Globe Theatre, Paul remarked, "They were in a very fortunate situation. Nobody had ever seen those plays before. What Burbage brought to them was obviously very satisfactory to the audiences of his time. If he found himself by magic 400 years later in London he would never get a chance to play all those parts. Today even spiffing actors are able to fail in the big roles but in Burbage's time no-one would know if he had failed as King Lear because they had never seen anybody else try it."

I had seen Paul Rogers several times on stage at the Old Vic in London during the 1950s. I particularly remember his Henry VIII in the 1952–53 season. It was a lively, spectacular production, directed by the late Sir Tyrone Guthrie, whom Paul admired as ". . . a stimulating, most wonderful man." There was something of the overgrown boy in Paul's Henry who was, as he colourfully expresses it, ". . . still young, and not the pox-ridden old bastard that he turned into! A monster, perhaps, but very much a child of his era." Gwen Ffrangcon-Davies was Queen Catherine, and the

117

Canadian actor Alexander Knox was a forceful Wolsey, with a hint of the butcher's son from Ipswich beneath the flowing red robes. The production had the unmistakable Guthrie touch.

Paul's admiration for Tyrone Guthrie as a director was confirmed by the exciting Old Vic production of *Troilus and Cressida* in which Paul played the assiduous go-between Pandarus. I saw it when it came to New York in 1956. In mentioning this to Paul I casually referred to the period in which the production had been set as '1912 Ruritania'. Paul pounced on this and said, "1912 yes, Ruritania *no*! It was done in 1912 because that was the very last moment in history when war was regarded as glorious. Why did I crack down on 'Ruritania'? Because it was all brilliantly arranged. The Trojans were the Austrian court with its affectations, and the Greeks were Prussians. Remember Achilles' myrmidons in their black shirts? I'm inclined to leap to Tony Guthrie's defence because too often people assume, because he was so gloriously light-hearted, because he was a man who rejoiced in the world and in his work, that he was flippant. He was *not*! He was a serious artist. He was capable at the same time of making people rejoice, and that is why I was so insistent that the actual nationalities employed were chosen with such care—the Austrians in their white uniforms, and the Prussians so like the Greeks. It was an amazing, wonderful choice. The period was not chosen in the spirit of 'How shall we do it, just to be different'." In this context Paul's Pandarus became, in Kenneth Tynan's words ". . . a Proustian voyeur."

Paul's second visit to Broadway was as Reginald Kinsale, the father in Peter Ustinov's ingenious play *Photo Finish* (subtitled 'An Adventure in Biography') at the Brooks Atkinson Theatre in 1963. Peter Ustinov, in his delightful autobiography *Dear Me*, praised Paul Rogers as ". . . the prototype of that extraordinary tradition of British character actors who have made a contribution to the reputation of the drama and cinema in Britain out of all proportion to their fame." Recalling his work with Paul in *Photo Finish* and in his film *Billy Budd*, Ustinov writes that he ". . . enriched my conscious-

Paul Rogers making up for the part of Max in The Homecoming
by Harold Pinter, at the Music Box Theatre, New York, 1967.

Paul Rogers as Max in The Homecoming.

ness of my profession as no-one else has done before or since."

My first meeting with Paul Rogers was in 1967 when he played Max in Harold Pinter's *The Homecoming* at the Music Box Theatre in New York, the part which won him a Tony Award for the Best Actor in a Drama. I had done a number of performance sketches and I had photostats made which I left for Paul at the stage door with a note saying that I would enjoy meeting him and drawing him 'as himself'.

I received a delightful letter in reply in which Paul said that he liked the sketches because they expressed ". . . just what I want an audience to get. A closer and longer scrutiny would only give the game away . . . that in fact my hands aren't the great butcher's hands I wanted you to feel as a participant in the play, and which to my great delight you have given Max. The thick brutality of the face is also very much a mutual effort of you and the character in performance. I love the drawings as they are. But, against my better judgement, if you would like to join me in my rat-hole of a dressing-room any day before the performance you will be very welcome."

He was cordial and communicative as I sketched him making up for the part of Max. His conversation was lively and entertaining and he has the quality that I have noticed in other British actors, of taking his *work* very seriously but not himself.

Eleven years later Paul was to give me a fascinating account of Harold Pinter's attitude during rehearsals for that production of *The Homecoming*. "That was an amazing experience. Pinter was there at almost all the rehearsals, at least when we got into London. We did a very long period in Stratford-on-Avon exploring the play. The one thing about Harold is, he will not pontificate or verbalize—he is the opposite. He loved being an actor himself—he was a damn good one—he loves to sit and see what the text is going to do. He is so aware that when he stops writing there are two further contributions to a playwright's work. One is the actor who creates the person; the other is the audience."

Vivien Merchant as Ruth, John Normington as Sam,
and Paul Rogers as Max in The Homecoming.

I asked whether Paul's concept of Max changed much in the course of rehearsals. He replied, "There was one moment when Harold did actually speak—it was very funny. In one scene Max described his father—how his father used to come home when Max was a baby, and how he and his friends would pick Max up, dandle him, toss him up high and all that sort of thing. . . . Going through the rehearsals—the family is Jewish and therefore a breadth of emotion somehow is allowed—it literally got to the point when tears of memory were streaming down my face! Eventually I took Harold by the lapels and I *shook* him. I said, 'What *do* you want?' And Harold just removed his glasses and said, 'He *hated* his father.' And then you get the picture of this baby, the terrible great ogres around him, and the smell of beer and whisky, and the horror of being picked up, and the terror of being thrown into the air and caught and—oh boy!—did it change! That's not only astute but honest. You see, there's an extraordinary honesty about Harold's writing; never for a moment does he slide into the trap of sentimentality. This was a remarkable experience. It was one of the great experiences of my life."

In 1968 Paul returned to Broadway in a musical at the Billy Rose Theatre based on the play *They Knew What They Wanted*. It was renamed *Here's Where I Belong*. "And it didn't," said Paul of the pleasant but unmemorable musical that closed after one night. I saw a preview, and the part of Adam Trask gave Paul the opportunity to sing, but little dramatic scope. He had a much longer run on Broadway in 1970 when he took over the part of Andrew Wyke in Anthony Shaffer's *tour-de-force*, the psychological thriller *Sleuth*. It remains one of Paul's favourite roles.

I regret all the more having missed Paul's King Lear at the Old Vic in 1958 having caught a tantalizing view of his handling of the part as 'Sir' in Ronald Harwood's entertaining and touching play *The Dresser*, which had its New York opening at the Brooks Atkinson Theatre in the winter of 1981. 'Sir' is an old-style actor-manager heading a seedy touring company in Britain during World War II. He is monstrously self-centred and rapidly disintegrating as a man yet utterly dedicated to his profession, reaching, one assumes, moments of sublimity as Lear.

The author, Ronald Harwood, was at one time Sir Donald Wolfit's dresser though he claims that 'Sir' is in no way intended to be a portrait of any one person but an amalgam of three or four such actor-managers. Paul commented, "It is accepted in the play that 'Sir' is a man who has elected, like so many of them, to be cock of his own walk, and who never actually got to London. Wolfit *did* get to London but very few of the touring actor-managers could make that jump. All those who did lost a fortune doing it. Matheson Lang lost *two* fortunes by the magnet of London, then had the good

Paul Rogers as 'Sir', with Tom Courtenay as Norman, in The Dresser
by Ronald Harwood, at the Brooks Atkinson Theatre, New York, 1981.

sense to go out into the provinces. He regained the lost fortune and
retired on it."

I had seen Wolfit's Lear in London in the 1950s and while his
performance had great moments it was obvious that, like 'Sir', he
had surrounded himself with lesser talent in a rather shabby production. I asked Paul if he would like to play Lear again. He replied,
"No, I don't think so. I was 41 when I played it. I am now 64." He
paused for a moment then said, "I suppose I would love to play
Lear, but what I don't want is to be subjected to other people's
preconceptions."

While I was chatting with Paul in his dressing-room after the
show a very serious young woman came in and wanted to know

if Paul used 'The Method'. He replied that he had studied for the stage at the Michael Chekhov Theatre Studio at Dartington Hall in Devon. I was interested to hear this as I had spent a weekend there many years ago and knew its director and guiding spirit, Mrs Dorothy Elmhurst and her daughter, the actress Beatrice Straight. I had also met Michael Chekhov briefly in Ridgefield, Connecticut, where he had moved his Theatre Studio after the outbreak of the Second World War.

I asked Paul about the Michael Chekhov experience when I visited him later in his apartment at the Gramercy Park Hotel. His wife Rosalind was there and all three of us had a long and relaxed conversation over coffee. Paul said, "Michael Chekhov was one of Stanislavsky's stars. He was a brilliant director and such was his quality that Stanislavsky set him up in his own theatre, the child of the Moscow Art Theatre. He was not only a disciple but, as it were, the very much loved artistic son of Stanislavsky."

I was curious about Paul's Hamlet, which he had played on a tour of Australia in 1957 with the Australian Elizabethan Theatre Trust Drama Company. Before discussing his own role Paul said, "Roz played the Queen. She got marvellous notices, from a poet in Sydney, a good playwright and a *very* perceptive critic." They laughed and Rosalind said, "The queen is not a heavy-weight, she is a light-weight, a *silly* woman—and Shakespeare was tormented by light women. Hamlet's attitude to Gertrude is protective. He knows her."

Of his Hamlet Paul said, "It was so long ago. But I feel that there are two things that are important. One is that there are two references in the text that put him at thirty—in the prologue to the play within the play ("Full thirty times hath Phoebus' cart gone round. . .") and in the gravedigger scene where Yorick's skull dates him exactly. He is *not* what Olivier calls him— '. . . a man who couldn't make up his mind'. He is an extremely adult, mature intellectual searcher. He has been to school at Wittenberg and wants to return there. We tend in Britain to think of 'school' as a place for juveniles but Wittenberg was then a dangerous place, full of heretical, subversive ideas.

The second point is that *Hamlet* is not only a play of deep philosophy, it is a play of deep religiosity—it is a deeply Catholic play. The king, villain though he may be, was an elected and anointed king. Hamlet has no right to the throne of Denmark—he says that Claudius has . . . come between the election and my *hopes'*. If you murder an anointed king you murder God! That's why I get very impatient with the casting of a juvenile. Hamlet is hyper-sensitive, yes, but he is a hyper-sensitive man of thirty. It is the sensitivity of the complete man and he was the complete Renaissance man until he was fixed by his terrible fate. Hamlet's problem is of such massive size. That was what I tried to do at the age of 41."

Paul always maintains the balance between inspiration and discipline, as is evident in his remark in our recent conversation: "The imagination is at once a very brilliant thing and a very dangerous thing. Acting at a certain level is not all that far away from madness—therefore you must be aware of where the line is drawn."